Preface

This book is published strictly for historical purposes. It provides the reader with a unique historical glimpse of Nazi propaganda tools utilized during 1934-1936 as the Nazi party was acquiring popularity and acceptance in pre-war Germany. It is not intended to be a glorification in any respect of the Nazi party, its members, its vile dogma or any of the heinous deeds carried out by the Nazi regime during the Second World War.

Reprinted and translated from a 1936 Edition
Copyright 1999 by Typhoon International

This translation of *Adolf Hitler* was prepared by a team of translators under the supervision of German Language Services in Seattle, Washington. The team endeavored to remain faithful to the German text and style. However, lengthy and convoluted German sentences have been rendered into shorter American-style sentences. We recognize that other strategies are also possible. Many thanks to the translators, editors, and proofreaders who enabled us to complete this difficult project in less than six weeks: Brian Buckner, Nina Gettler, Jeff Nadeau, Anne Quinn, Alexandra Scott, Nicole Teuber, Karen Williams, and Sarah Williams. We hope that the reader will find the result an interesting window into the time of Hitler's rise to power.

Courtney Searls-Ridge
Director, German Language Services
Seattle, Washington

Printed in Croatia
ISBN 1 582 79031 0

Adolf Hitler

PICTURES FROM THE LIFE OF THE FÜHRER

301–400 Thousand
Heinrich Hoffmann, NSDAP Press Photographer of the Reich, Munich, was responsible for the
selection and artistic arrangement of the photographs in this work.
The full-page front piece is a reproduction of a painting by B. Jacobs.
Binding and title page designed by O.H.W. Hadank, Berlin
Graphic Design: Carl Ernst Poeschel, Leipzig

We are unable to express our gratitude in words, my Führer. Nor are we able to find the words to demonstrate our loyalty and affection for you. All the gratitude, love, and passionate faith in you, my Führer, shines upon you today from a hundred thousand eyes. An entire Volk, an entire nation, is strong and happy today because these people have found in you more than a Führer; they have also found a savior.

Göring

The Reichstag President at the German Reichstag in Nuremberg on September 15, 1935

Table of Contents

	Page
Foreword by Dr. Joseph Goebbels	7
The Führer's Travels by SS Generalmajor Julius Schreck †	9
The Führer and the German People by Dr. Otto Dietrich	19
The Führer as an Orator by Dr. Joseph Goebbles	27
The Private Life of the Führer by General Wilhelm Brückner	35
The Führer as Statesman by Dr. Joseph Goebbels	44
The Führer and the German Worker by Dr. Robert Ley	56
The Führer and the Arts by Dr. Joseph Goebbels	64
The Buildings of the Führer by Albert Speer, Architect	72
Adolf Hitler and His Roads by Inspector General Fritz Todt, Doctor of Engineering	78
Our Hitler (radio speech to the German nation on the Führer's birthday) by Dr. Joseph Goebbels	85
The Führer and the Wehrmacht by First Lieutenant Foertsch	91
The Führer and German Youth by Baldur von Schirach	105
Special contribution by SS General Major Julius Schaub, The Führer in Landsberg Prison	126

Foreword

Many misunderstandings still prevail – throughout the world and even in Germany – on the concept of propaganda. Since these misconceptions are so ingrained and for the most part based on prejudices, they are difficult to clear up. Since the end of the war, the German nation in particular has been taught an object lesson on this subject. It is impossible to imagine a better or more powerful lesson. In a relatively short time span historically, propaganda has become extremely important in Germany; today there is more than enough proof of the fact that imperial Germany was overthrown by the onset of Marxist propaganda. It is also clear that the Marxist-democratic regime was overcome solely because the idea of National Socialism and National Socialist propaganda countered Marxism with a superior new order and efficiency.

Even propaganda must be mastered. It is absolutely useless to assign this job to just any bright person who happens to be available as the need arises. As with all great art, it requires uniquely qualified people who usually found a school through which they render their art form acceptable. The common misconception that propaganda is dishonorable or inferior must also be dispelled. As with everything else in life, it depends entirely on how it is used and what it contributes in practical terms to the world. In this sense, propaganda has nothing at all to do with promotion. At its best, propaganda allows situations and people to speak for themselves. Propaganda ensures that if something is worthwhile, its full value is brought to light and explained.

Good things and great people speak for themselves. One must value them and not place restrictions on them. The most important characteristic of particularly successful propaganda is that nothing is omitted and nothing is added that is not essential to the subject in question. The characteristics of situations or personalities are to be clearly, powerfully, simply, and naturally lifted out of the confusion of current topics, so that these points are understandable and obvious to the masses of people who shall be moved and won over.

National Socialism and its principal representatives lend themselves naturally to this art. And they have worked hard to learn and apply their art. They have accomplished this through untiring and extremely close contact with the people and by progressively refining their skills to the highest level. Moreover, the Führer himself was the greatest teacher of propaganda. It is a little-known fact that for quite a while early in the history of the party the Führer held no office other than that of Director of Propaganda.

His ingenious mastery and management of this office left upon the party a unique intellectual, organizational, and political mark.

From the very beginning his supporters (and later the entire German nation) focused the entirety of their love on him and placed an enormous store of trust in him, for his very nature and character recognized the necessity of speaking to his people (whose child he always was and always will be) and of acting from the heart. Initially the masses saw him from a distance only as a politician and statesman. The purely human side of him remained in many ways in the background.

Today the world recognizes Hitler as the creator of National Socialist doctrine and the organizer of the National Socialist state; as the pioneer of a new European order; as the guide to peace and to the welfare of nations. But untold millions all over the world know that behind all of this there is the exciting and fascinating figure of the man Adolf Hitler – even if they have only a rough idea of what this means. The great simplicity and the simple greatness radiating from his person completely and compellingly affect not only every German, but also touch every foreigner who possesses good instincts. Today he can no doubt be described the world over as the man who is most deeply and clearly rooted in the thought and mood of these modern times, and who because of this, has within himself the ability to reform these times as no other can.

In order to completely appreciate this side of him, one must see him as a person in addition to politician and statesman. And this book shall be a guide. This book provides insight into his personality, brought with love and veneration from his closest colleagues and oldest comrades. In this book, the authors offer the public a picture of this great man that has not previously been seen. All of the contributors to this publication have known the Führer for many years, right down to the last detail, and thus have come to admire him more and more each day. It is this perspective that makes this book valuable.

The Führer appears in this book as a person with an immediate connection to all the issues of our times. The German nation will gladly grasp this chance to see the Führer up close, thereby getting closer to him personally.

In addition, it is particularly gratifying that this book will be easily available and affordable. This will give masses of German readers access to it. May this book hereby begin its felicitous and successful path to the German people!

Dr. Joseph Goebbels

The Führer promotes aviation by example.

The Führer's Travels

By SS Brigade Captain Julius Schreck †

Never before has a prominent statesman become so thoroughly acquainted with his country and people as Adolf Hitler. Whether by automobile, airplane, or train, his travels always promote a thorough acquaintance with his nation. Even at the beginning of his movement, he had the foresight to recognize the importance of rapid transportation, particularly the automobile; he utilized rapid transportation despite his quite modest means at that time. Today the Führer still prefers the automobile because it is important to him to remain in constant contact with his comrades and old campaigners.

The great political battles for power proved that the Führer was far ahead of all his adversaries due to the motorization of his retinue. At that time, there were not always throngs of cheering people surrounding the Führer. During the campaign years we experienced some trips that were very difficult, and we were only able to secure a path by using presence of mind and force. No reports of trouble ahead could prevent the Führer from driving into the strongholds of red and black adversaries (often right through the middle of wild crowds of Bolsheviks) and past the demonstrations of the other side. Sometimes our car was completely surrounded by thousands of incited comrades. But time after time we experienced how their raised fists sank under the gaze of the Führer, how they looked up and realized that this Hitler looked quite different than he had always been described to them. How many misguided German workers looked then for the first time into the eyes of the man who was supposed to be their adversary, only to become fanatical supporters of his Movement right then and there? No newspaper propaganda, no books alone could have accomplished this marvel. And thus three years after he seized power he was able to say, "Where else is there a statesman like myself who, after three years of governing, does not have to fear going out among the people – just as I did back then?"

To this very day when his work and government business allow him, rather than staying in his office, the Führer drives out into the country to be among the people. Once again he sits in his Mercedes and makes appearances here and there. One day

The Führer in Franconia. At the war memorial in Hiltpoltstein (known as Franconian Switzerland).

Trip through a small Franconian town.

he will be in the Ruhr District, the next in Baden, Württemberg, Saxony, East Prussia, or on the coast. In short, there is no region to which he has not journeyed at one time or another. Sitting at the steering wheel behind the windshield I suddenly hear amazed and enthusiastic cries such as "it's Hitler!" or "the Führer is here!" Often people do not even notice who has just driven through the city. Not until the convoy has passed do the three black cars attract attention.

And then, all of the sudden, they realize who has just driven by. The children are usually the first to see the Führer. Then a race begins with the car, and more often than not people

be able to share these days with him.

The Führer takes major trips only in open cars, which he leaves open during official business even when it rains. He always has the same response to the advice of his entourage, "As long as the SA men and other formations have to stand in the rain, then we can also get wet." Thousands of people witnessed how he, hatless and in a brown shirt with no coat, reviewed the SA march at the reintegration of the Saar; how he spoke to the waiting crowd in the pouring rain during the election campaigns in Stralsund following a night flight at three o'clock in the morning; and how he drove in the rain through Holstein to the Adolf Hitler Polder, soaked, without thinking of himself, because the SA men also stood in the rain.

Even in his first car he sat beside his driver. Today, fifteen years later, as Chancellor of the Reich, he still sits next to his driver.

In his travels through Germany, the Führer prefers an open car.

are quick to gather because the news has spread through the streets. We often end up stopping so that the Führer can shake hands with enthusiastic supporters, accept flowers, or sign a few cards.

Anyone who has had the luck to be near the Führer constantly for ten straight years, as I have been, and to experience his many trips with him will never forget the thousands of sights seen over the years. One comes away from these trips with an irrepressible faith in the German nation, and it is often quite heartwarming to

On a trip through Germany.

Julius Schreck, died May 16, 1936

The National Socialist German Worker's Party
bids farewell to Julius Schreck

The National Socialist Movement bids farewell today to Julius Schreck. It bids farewell to one of its oldest and most loyal members. It bids farewell to one of its best and most irreplaceable members. It bids farewell to one of its most unassuming members, one who wanted nothing for himself and gave everything for Germany and the Führer.

When called upon to fight for Germany he stood at the front, abroad during the World War, as well as at home.

His veneration and love for the Führer were boundless. His concern for the Führer indefatigable, his consideration for the protection of the Führer judicious.

His essence radiated faithfulness to the end. His presence spread a feeling of security among his party comrades in difficult times of conflict.

His judgment of people was faultless; his affection was unconcealed, as were his aversions. A tough old soldier with a warm heart. Feared by his adversaries, loved by all who counted him as one of them, admired as a fatherly friend by his subordinates.

He had the good fortune of enjoying his Führer's deepest trust. The movement lowers its flags to pay its last respects to Julius Schreck. It thereby vows to him that his manner and spirit will be a model to the youth and to future generations, through which he shall serve the movement far into the future for the benefit of our great National Socialist Germany.

Rudolf Hess

Trip through the Harz Mountains. The Führer can also be light-hearted.

A break in the forest.

On a trip

In the German countryside. Hiltpoltstein (known as Franconian Switzerland)

The Führer sets the travel route.

The Führer in an airplane

He also sets the travel route himself, for the Führer loves to use side streets and to experience Germany's countryside away from the main traffic routes.

It used to be simpler, when the Führer was not yet as well known as he is today. Back then it was sometimes possible to spend the night in an inn or to have a meal without being recognized. Today it's different. News of the Führer's approach spreads through the villages and cities along our way like a brush fire. Many people joyfully pass on the news to the next village by telephone. Then the residents of the town, who have never seen their Führer, start waiting to greet Hitler when his car arrives. These are uplifting moments, and sometimes you wish you were a poet so as to find the words that adequately describe the thousand little occurrences as we experience them. Here we come through a town. Everyone is there, young and old, clubs and schools, mothers with children in their arms. The street through town quickly becomes a sea of flags. Members of the League of German Girls try to bring the car to a stop, but time is of the essence and the Führer must reach his destination at a specific time, for hundreds of thousands wait for him at the scheduled assembly. Then a big muscular man jumps onto the car's radiator in one bound – it is the town's blacksmith. Now the driver must slow down, and before you know it the car is surrounded by all of the town's residents. Everyone wants to shake the Führer's hand. Women holding children are not able to approach. They hold their little ones, Germany's future, high above the enthusiastic crowd, as if to say "you belong to him!"

In order to describe great men, you must also see the small things. Here is one of hundreds of episodes. It is around 10 o'clock at night as the Führer's car is driving toward Würzburg after a parade in Meiningen. There, in the headlights, are two marching SA men. The Führer orders the car to be stopped. Where do they want to go, they are asked. "To the next train station. My comrade can no longer walk and we still have three hours to go." "Well, get in the car!" They have no idea whose guests they are. We ask them about this and that. Whether they have seen the Führer yet? "Yes, today at the parade." The car stops; we have reached the destination. The Führer, who is sitting in front, calls them and hands each a gift of money. There, in the dark of the night, a small beam of light falls on the Führer's face. Both of the SA men stare. Is that not the Führer who is speaking to them? Yes, it is! They are too joyful and shocked to speak. I hit the gas, and the Mercedes takes off into the dark night. As we go around a bend we see the two still standing on the country road motionless under the effect of what they have just experienced.

The great and difficult election campaigns of that time required that the Führer make the most of his time, and so he also traveled by air. That was a time when

At Wartburg

people still distrusted airplanes. For weeks on end he would fly from city to city without regard for wind or weather.

Looking back, it's a bit frightening to remember the many flights in storms, at night, or in fog. It really says something that the Führer's departure was never once postponed when he used the plane during the election campaign. Every scheduled rally started on time – and sometimes there were four or five in different German cities in one day.

Often the Führer was urged not to take one flight or another. But his answer was always, "I will fly whenever necessary, even in a storm." How the opposition newspapers would have loved it if the set flight plan had been delayed or if a scheduled rally had been canceled. But Hitler did not do them this favor.

One flight from Fürth to Frankfurt particularly stands out in my memory. The old Rohrbach, the first plane the Führer used back then, was anchored with gasoline drums. An unusually intense storm raged across all of Germany. Takeoff restrictions applied for general air traffic. Only with effort could you stay on your feet. Everyone shook his head as the Führer boarded the

Above Nuremberg in a D-2600. Arrival at the 1934 National Socialist Party Congress.

Campaign trip through Germany.

plane. Yet a few minutes later, it was fighting its way up. The machine's forward progress was laborious, through thunderstorms and squalls, wind and snow. The plane often pitched downward, so that the heads of some of the passengers hit the ceiling, but it went well throughout. Once the plane had to make an emergency landing far away from its final destination. The assembly was set to begin in Kiel at eight o'clock. At five o'clock, I received news that the Führer had had to land in Travemünde due to low

17

clouds, fog, and the worst of the storm.

The convoy immediately roared off in the direction of Lübeck. Somewhere near Eutin we were able to meet the Führer traveling toward us in a rented car, and we were still able to get him to Kiel on time.

Even though the Führer uses the train now and then for overnight travel in order to save time, his great love is still the automobile, which he once said had revealed Germany to him. And he equally loves his Ju 52 under the command of Flight Captain SS Colonel Baur, who no doubt ranks as one of the foremost masters among flight captains. The most enjoyable activity for the Führer is driving through the German countryside in his car after weeks of strenuous work. The greatest days for me are when I am allowed to sit behind the wheel to drive the Führer through the fortunate, peaceful country as I once did through battle and hardship.

At Bückeberg for the 1934 harvest festival.

Women of Bückeberg in their festive costumes at the 1934 harvest festival.

While traveling through East Prussia, the Führer visits a farmer and his family.

The Führer and the German People
By Dr. Otto Dietrich

The relationship of the German people to the Führer has always been a source of joyous pride for the Germans and a source of amazement for foreigners. Nowhere in the world is there such fanatic love of millions of people for one man – a love which despite everything is not exaggerated or frenzied, but which arises from a deep and great devotion, an infinite trust, like the trust children sometimes place in a very good father.

Infatuation lasts a few years, but once love from the heart of hearts has bloomed, it is indestructible and lasts for centuries. It is like a great, powerful light that never dims. This love did not flare up suddenly. It was not sparked by unexpected or stirring events, but it has grown slowly and insistently. It does not break free with a raging impetuousness at some single occasion, but it is always there at every moment and within every German, whether at occasions that fill his heart with pride, whether he is standing with hundreds of thousands of other comrades in front of the Führer, or whether there is no special occasion at all and he is simply quiet and alone at his work. Always, whenever anyone thinks of the Führer, this deep love swells up from within. This love alone justifies the words: "Hitler is Germany – Germany is Hitler." Never has a man been closer to the hearts of the people than this man, who himself has come from the people. He is not an outsider, but was born one of the people. He has felt the deprivation of the people, and he has lived the life of the people. If today someone were to ask the name of the unknown German soldier, the whole German nation would answer: Adolf Hitler!

He was the conscience of the nation. The suffering and the defiance of a downtrodden nation cried out from his lips and in him the will of all of Germany to live became word and deed in the hour of the country's deepest humiliation. Adolf Hitler has never said a word that the nation was not thinking in its heart of hearts. He has never done anything that the entire nation did not want to do. He was not, is not, and never will be a dictator forcing his personal opinion or his desire for power upon the nation. He really is just the Führer, and that is the highest praise one can give any man.

It is because of this that the people love him so, why they trust him, why they are so indescribably happy to have found themselves in this man for the first time in history.

Herein lies the secret of the indestructibility of Adolf Hitler and his work – the guarantee that the road he has taken can not be altered. For it is no longer the man Adolf Hitler, it is no longer his works and no longer the road he has taken that expresses itself in him. It is the German nation itself that expresses itself in him. In him the nation loves itself, in him it follows its most secret desires, in him its most daring thoughts become reality. Every single person feels this and because of it Adolf Hitler is a stranger to no one, and no one is a stranger to the Führer. Workers and farmers speak with him; Nobel prize winners and artists, warriors and dreamers, happy men and despairing men speak with him, and each and every one hears his own language, he understands and is understood in return. Everything is natural and self-evident, and no one is shy before this great man. No one is ordered to follow. No one is courted, but everyone is called, just as one would be called by his own conscience. He has no choice but to follow, should he not want to be guilty and unhappy in his own heart. Thus, what must happen happens voluntarily, and no nation on the face of this earth has more freedom than the Germans.

And so the nation does not tire of listening to the words of the Führer, and even if the party assembly in Nuremberg were twice as long, the people would stand there on the last day and listen to him as raptly as they listened on the first. He could travel constantly throughout Germany and the people would wait alongside the roads day in and day out cheering him as they had on the very first day. They would bring him their children so that he could see the future of Germany.

On the day of the reunion with the Saar

Enthusiasm for the Führer's presence at the Hamburg docks

Delegation from the Saar region in front of the chancellery

She wants the Führer's hand.

Everyone wants to shake the Führer's hand.

The farmers, too, believe in the Führer.

And if they had to, they would give their lives, just as hundreds of his party comrades did in the years of the struggle.

There have been emperors and kings, sovereigns and popular heroes; usurpers and terrorists, wise and great rulers leading nations; but there has never been simply: the Führer. This is unique in the whole world, and it is an amazing stroke of luck for the German nation. Without understanding this, one can understand nothing about the German people. One will not understand why eyes sparkle, why voices cry out, why arms wave in the air, why hearts beat faster when Adolf Hitler stands in front of the German people. And from these external signs, which merely make visible the constant and mysterious affinity between the nation and the Führer, Hitler draws strength for new works, just as the people draw strength from the sight of him.

This becomes especially clear when German youth and the Führer are face to face. Anyone who has been with the Führer for any period of time, who has accompanied him for days and weeks and months, has a store of unforgettable images.

One time between Stettin and Pasewalk, a good ten kilometers from any town, a group of young Germans stood in storm and rain in the middle of a country road because they had heard from somewhere that the Führer would be coming along this road today. Day turned to evening, and when the Führer's car with its two escort cars raced along the road you could see a throng far ahead among the trees lining the road. Drawing closer, you could see that the throng was a crowd of children waving flags. They were burning red, blue, and green sparklers, and they had set up guards ahead of the main group to stop the convoy with hand signals. Although time was short, the Führer gave the order to stop, and immediately the car was surrounded by about a hundred children who jumped on the running boards and crawled up on the radiators and hoods in order to peer through the windshields to try and find the Führer.

The older generation trusts the Führer.

After they had well and truly examined all three cars, a particularly clever boy finally discovered the Führer. He shouted as loud as he could, "Here he is. Everyone come here!" And then the fuss began. The escorting commando had to intervene because some of the boys even tried to climb onto the shaky canvas roof. The leader of the group, the same boy who had first seen the Führer, gave a brief speech – youthful, bright and innocent. And then everyone stepped back to make room for a girl dressed all in white. She curtsied low and recited some verses she had written about how happy the young people were to see the Führer. Finally, she presented Adolf Hitler with a small basket of wonderful, red apples. Deeply touched, the Führer stroked her blond hair, and the girl – overwrought with joy and happiness – suddenly began to cry. Slowly the line of cars eased away from the crowd of children, and for a long time you could see through the rear windshield the small figures waving their flags in farewell.

Always and at all the assemblies it is the youth that stands in the front rows. The well behaved, modest ones stay just as the teachers or the standard bearer places them, straight as an arrow, all in a row, without moving an inch. Others, more daring, hang from the limbs of trees, sit on monuments and building cornices, or stand like a line of living statues on high factory walls. They populate flagpoles and lantern posts, and when the Führer passes by they fill the air with their cries of joy. A favorite place for the young people to wait for the Führer is in front of the curves, where they set themselves up so cleverly that the cars are forced to drive as slowly as possible. An even better place is a construction site on a secondary road, for they are sure that here the Führer will have to drive by at a walking pace, and that they will certainly be able to catch him. It almost always takes quite a bit of effort to get away because whenever the road in front of the car seems clear, the cheering children run from the back of the car to the front and block the way again.

Once in a city in southern Germany on the evening of one of the Führer's assemblies, tens of thousands of Hitler Youth members lined the streets. The wider the road became the closer the rows of boys moved, so that eventually there was just enough room for the car to pass. At first everything went well. But then suddenly people began to run, to jostle, to push. At first the youthful torch-bearers in the front row tried to hold back the onslaught, but then they were pushed along, running, swinging their torches, and lighting up the interior of the cars. Because of this sheer enthusiasm and love the Führer and his escort ended up swallowing large amounts of smoke. It was fortunate that the cars were not set on fire.

It took a good quarter of an hour to free the Führer from this enthusiastic crowd of youngsters.

It is interesting to see the seriousness and eagerness with which young people try to photograph the Führer. They stand with their tiny cameras, their fingers on the shutter release, trembling with nervousness and excitement. Obviously they need a lot of luck to be able to get a picture at all with these cameras. And yet we find a good likeness in an amazing number of these photographs. Even here, luck seems to be on the side of youth because more experienced amateur photographers often complain that they simply cannot get a good opportunity for a picture because of the general enthusiasm and crush of people around the Führer.

While traveling through Upper Selesia, the Führer is welcomed by a small town, and a little girl has the honor of presenting him with a bouquet of flowers. She is supposed to recite a brief poem, and she manages to get the first line out without faltering. But then in her excitement she loses the thread and after looking around several times helplessly, she takes the flowers, stretches up on her tiptoes toward the Führer, presses the flowers into his hands and says, "H-h-hitler, here you are, f-f-f-forgot everything!" and runs off.

There is a street. It is closed off and people are crowded close together. They are waiting, some for hours. They are waiting for the Führer. They want to see him. Everyone wants to see him, men and women, boys and girls. "It is like a holiday today," says an old woman. And she is right, for today the Führer is coming to this little town for the first time.

Flags flutter from rooftops, and gables and garlands are strung across the streets. The whole town is decorated. And then the Führer arrives – a whirlwind seems to pass through the crowd. Here and there ripples appear in the long line of the security troops, people begin to jostle and push,

A picture taken during the 1932 election in Hesse.

arms are raised toward the Führer, there is laughter and tears, both expressing joy and enthusiasm. The women hold up their children whose little arms rise above the crowd. With sparkling eyes and smiles, they add their voices to the enthusiastic cries of "Heil Hitler." The women look at the Führer and are filled with optimism and trust. They know that they have only him to thank that their unemployed husbands have found work and can provide food for the family. Finally, life has meaning once again. They can look to the future without fear and dread.

There is a letter that a girl doing her compulsory year on a farm wrote to her parents: ". . . I must start another page. What I am going to write now is bound to make you happy. Imagine, my dears, I have seen the Führer, imagine that, the Führer!" What sentiments are expressed in these four words: "Imagine that, the Führer!" How her pride for what she has experienced shines through, how great is the love of this child of the German nation for her Führer! Here is the fulfillment of a wish that this girl probably never even had the courage to express.

This is a real gift of fate. Fate gave her the ultimate gift in the midst of her agricultural service year, a meeting with the Führer. "Imagine what that means . . .!"

And this is the way it is everywhere – in Bavaria and East Prussia, in Silesia and in the Rheinland.

On a Palatine country road two workers are walking to the next town. The work camp is way out in the country a long way from the railroad station. But both men are cheerful and whistling because they are going home on leave after months of healthy, hard work. They are whistling, "In the homeland, in the homeland. . ." Just then a line of cars races past the two men. "They have it good," one of them says. "They're faster than we are," says the other one. "They're waving!" cry out both in unison. And the line of cars actually stops and waits until the men, who are running by now, have reached it. "Where are you coming from? Where are you going? Get in!" Both men are wide-eyed with amazement when they see that it is the Führer who has stopped on a country road and invited two camp workers to get in. He asks them all about their lives, and he wants to know every detail of what it is like in the work camp. Then they reach the small town. The cars stop. As they leave, the Führer says to one of them, "It is about to rain.

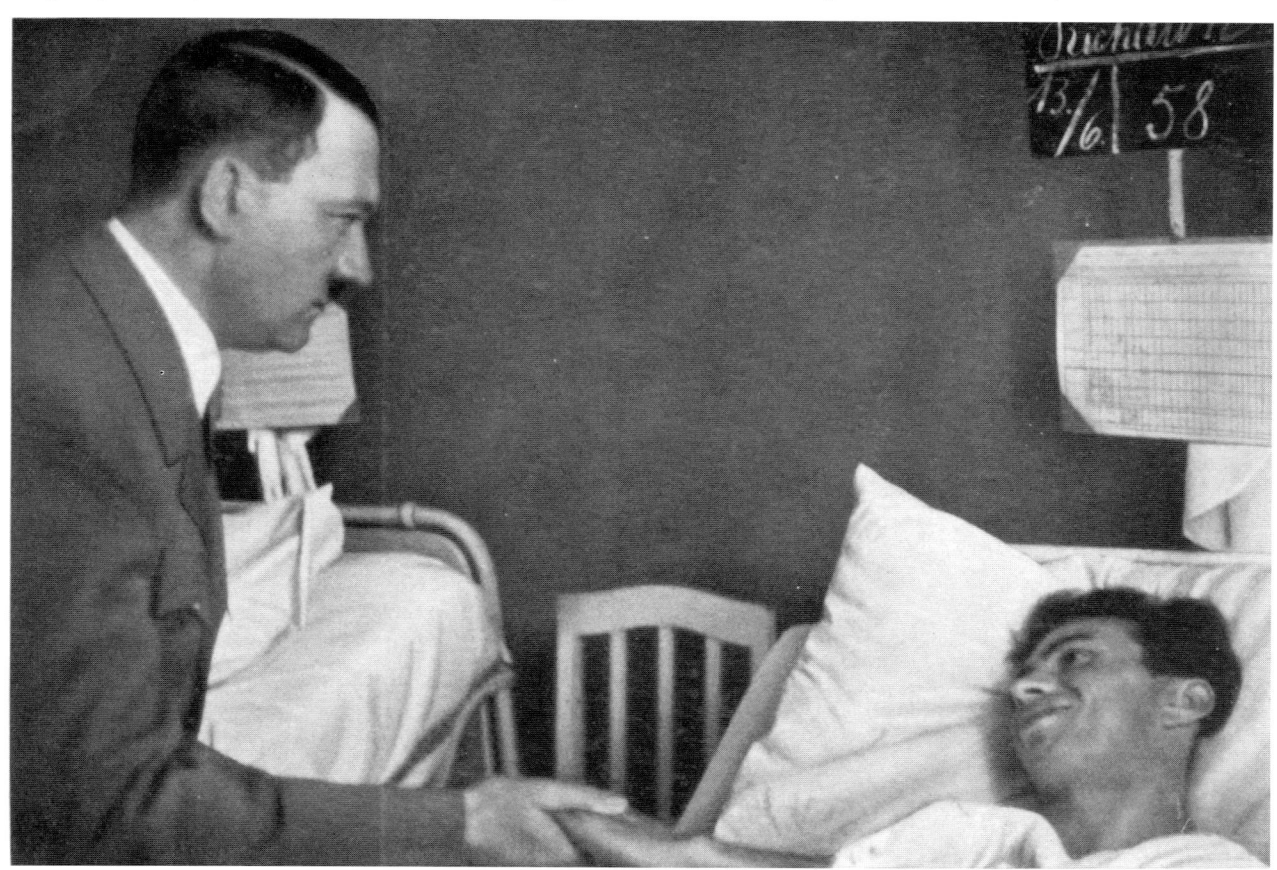

Visiting the Reinsdorf victims

Don't you have a coat?" "I don't have a civilian coat, my Führer. I was unemployed for a long time." Then the Führer takes off his gray traveling coat and puts it around the shoulders of his comrade. And before the man can say a word of thanks, the procession of cars races off into the distance.

Somewhere a group of young factory workers lines up for roll call. The Führer inspects the row and looks deep into the eyes of each young man. He addresses one. "Are you a member of the party?" – "No!" – "Are you an SA man?" – "No, I belong to the Labor Front." – "Where were you before?" the Führer asks after a brief pause. The young blond man lowers his gaze, then he straightens up and says hesitantly, "I belonged to the Communist Youth, my Führer!" It is obviously difficult for him to speak. Everyone's gaze is upon him. An embarrassing moment. But the Führer takes the young man's hand, holds it, and says, "But today you are all with me, my boys." And blushing, the young worker answers, "By God, you can depend on that, my Führer!"

So many images – all bearing witness to the closeness each German feels to Adolf Hitler.

In Hamburg at one of the Führer's assemblies, on the evening before a decisive plebiscite, a seriously disabled war veteran with his son pushes past the chains closing off the entrance to the Führer's quarters. "I want to serenade the Führer." The SS men let the veteran through. He stands under the Führer's window. Hands trembling, he removes his instrument from its gray case and plays a song. The crowd of many thousands listens quietly and reverently. The plaintive melodies search out the Führer. And the Führer hears the music. The Führer has the man brought to him, speaks to him, and listens to the story of his life. "I have been unemployed for four years now," the disabled man finally says. "My Führer, can you find a way for me earn a wage and provide food for my family again?" The Führer waves to one of his aides. Two quick telephone calls later the Führer says, "Report tomorrow to such and such and you can begin work immediately." The news spreads as if on wings throughout the waiting crowd. Loud ovations that seem endless swell up in the direction of the Führer.

Another unforgettable day was when the Führer went to the funeral of the victims of a catastrophic explosion in Reinsdorf. The coffins of the fallen heroes of the work camp were lined up in a long row. Flags fluttered at half-mast, mourners with black ribbons stood silently. The victims' next of kin were gathered in a section apart. The weeping mothers, sisters, brothers, and fathers were a picture of deep sadness. Then the Führer appeared, and the funeral began. The pain of the survivors was heartbreaking. Various speakers and clergymen spoke, the song about the good comrade was played, and the sound of the salute rolled across the field. Leaving his escort behind, the Führer crossed the square to where the relatives stood. A hundred arms stretched out to him, seeking comfort. Everyone who was there will remember the sorrowful face of the Führer as he stood in the midst of this infinite grief. He spoke with some of the men and women or simply shook their hands silently. The circle around him tightened, tears stopped flowing, and despairing mourners straightened up. The Führer grasped between his comforting hands the head of an inconsolable old woman who had lost her son. He heartened a deathly pale boy in a Hitler Youth

A picture taken during the 1932 election in Hesse

uniform who had lost his father. The comfort that the Führer gave these mourners was so powerful because they felt that they were not alone in their grief. When finally the mourning relatives raised their arms to silently thank Adolf Hitler one more time, Führer and people were close, even in this time of deep sadness.

The Führer and the German people – at a rally once in the Frankfurter Festhalle, while the Führer spoke to thousands, a woman crept to his car and put a tiny bouquet of lilies-of-the-valley (it was the middle of winter) on the seat where she believed the Führer would sit. As the line of cars began to drive away after the rally, from the middle of the swell of shouts of "Heil," came a high, piercing voice, "The lilies-of-the-valley are from me!"

There are hundreds and thousands of these stories to be told, touching and amusing. They all express one single sentiment: that a miracle has taken place here, such as a nation can experience but once in its whole history; that here Führer and people are one and the same; and that the love that binds the people and their Führer is so great, so natural, so self-evident that it constantly flares up anew, as sparkling and as strong as before.

What infinite strength, what eternal blessings blossom from this love for both the people and the Führer – for the Führer and the German nation!

Minister Dareé greets the Führer at a thanksgiving celebration.

November 9, 1934 in Munich. The Führer speaks at the Feldherrnhalle to newly recruited members of the Hitler Youth and the League of German Girls.

The Führer as an Orator
by Dr. Joseph Goebbles

There are two types of orators. They are fundamentally different in nature: one speaks from his intellect and the other from his heart. And respectively, they appeal to two different types of people: those who listen with their minds and those who listen with their hearts. Usually those who speak from the intellect come out of the parliament; those who speak from the heart are born of the people.

If he wants to speak effectively, an orator who speaks from the intellect must be able to quote statistics and a large number of facts. He must master dialectics as a pianist masters the keyboard. He builds his train of thought with cold, calculated logic and draws from it his inevitable conclusions. In general he reaches people who operate primarily from – or only from – the intellect. This type of orator is not a great, sweeping success. He does not know how to stir up the masses or how to encourage them toward great, far-reaching goals. He is limited to the purely instructional.

He is ice cold, and he leaves his listeners just as cold. At best he can convince people, but he can never mobilize the masses or to get them to march into action while setting their own needs aside – even less so when they are facing danger and death.

The orator who speaks from the heart is different. This is not to say that he has not mastered the skills of the intellectual speaker. As a true virtuoso of oration, in many ways these skills are just tools for him to use as he desires. Far beyond this though, he uses abilities that the intellectual speaker will never have available: clarity in diction goes hand-in-hand with the effective simplicity with which he puts thoughts together, making them easy to understand; he senses instinctively what should be said and how it should be said. When this type of orator speaks, a great poetic performance comes together with monumental ideas. This orator knows the most mysterious wrinkles and ramifications of the soul of the masses. He knows how to expose and stir these ramifications with the hand of a master. His speeches are works of art in rhetoric. In epic style he describes people and situations; with a sharp stone tool he writes his thesis on the slates of time; with great and noble pathos he carefully builds the towering columns of his world view. His voice comes from deep within his blood, penetrating deep into the veins of his listeners. His voice sounds the most mysterious chords in the human soul. It rouses the sluggish and lazy; it makes the indifferent and doubtful stand straight; it transforms cowards into men and weaklings into heroes.

Only seldom in history have such voices been heard. But if they are mighty enough to penetrate this sluggish century, they will surely change the conditions and the course of nations.

The Führer with Hierl, the Head of the Labor Front, speaking to 47,000 workers at the National Socialist Party assembly in 1935.

These rhetorical geniuses beat the drums of destiny. Historically they begin alone in times of despair and collapse. And suddenly and unexpectedly they are in the center of the bright spotlight of something new. These are the orators who shape a nation's history.

Like every great speaker, the orator who speaks from the heart has his own individual style. He can only be himself. He is what he says. His language matches his essence and his style, whether this language is being used in a proclamation, on a placard, in a letter or article, or in an address or a speech.

There are many examples perfectly demonstrating throughout history that the only similarity among great orators is the greatness of their achievements. Their appeal to nations and their appeal to the heart will always differ according to the times, the nation, and the character of the epoch. Caesar spoke differently to his legions than Friedrich the Great to his grenadiers. Napoleon spoke differently to his guard than Bismarck to the members of the Prussian parliament. Each used language that the men in front of him would understand. Each used words and thoughts that set off sparks in men's minds and resonated in their hearts. These orators gave vivid expression to the deepest and most puzzling daemon of their times, thereby serving as eternal beacons of enduring ideas across the centuries. They made history and shaped nations.

It also seems that different races have different predispositions to oratory, as if there are some who are too reserved for this electrifying craft,

Speaking to the workers at Blohm & Voß.

Taking over the Leadership School in Bernau in 1933.

The Führer running for election for Germany's freedom. March, 1936.

whereas others seem to be plainly predestined for it. The Romans were known for their oratory skills for good reason. The great wealth of general and notable rhetorical talents of the Romance peoples to some extent justifies this reputation. And this is also why the gift of oratory has an effect on a public that understands this gift, holds onto it, and gives it the most opportunity to have an impact.

Throughout history, our German nation has not done well in this respect. We have produced an abundance of statesmen and soldiers, philosophers and scientists, musicians and poets, architects and engineers, planning and organizational geniuses. But we have always lacked great rhetorical talents. After Fichte's classical speeches to the German nation there was no one else able to warm the hearts of the people until Bismarck. After Bismarck left the speaker's podium, there was no one else who could speak effectively until a new beacon arose in response to public need after the collapse following the World War. Everything in between was at best mediocre, adequate for domestic policies in parliament or for the corporate board room; but such was met with icy reserve by the people, who were in need of someone to reach them at their deepest level.

This had also to do with the time in history – a time of no great ideas or grand projects. Rhetoric declined into a dull feeling of satiety. The only apparent exception, Marxism, was secretly representing materialism, which will never set off the spark of true genius.

But revolutions breed true orators, and true orators create revolutions! One should not overestimate the role of the written or printed word. The spoken word, on the other hand, kindles the minds and hearts of people with the secret magic of its immediate impact. The eyes and ears register the spoken word; those who are still wavering and confused are drawn irresistibly into the spell cast by the force of the masses of people who have already been reached by the sound of a human voice.

What would become of a genius statesman if fate made him inferior, denying him from the beginning the power of speech and the explosive power of the word? This power allows him to create ideas from ideals and to create reality from ideas. With its help, people who are prepared to fight for these ideas gather around his flag; compelled, men risk health and life to lead a new world into victory. From the propaganda of the word, an organization forms; from the organization, a movement develops; and that movement conquers the state. It's not a matter of whether ideas are right. The key is to bring them to the masses so that the masses support them.

Theories will always be theories if people do not act on them. But in difficult times people will only answer a call that ignites their hearts if the call also comes from the heart.

It is hard to categorize the Führer as a orator. His art of molding the masses is so amazing and unique that it fits no pattern or dogma. It would be absurd to think that he had attended an oratorical or language school; he is a genius at speaking, entirely self-taught with no help from anyone. It is hard to imagine that the Führer ever spoke any differently than he now does, or that he ever will. He says what comes to him from his heart, and what he says goes directly to the heart of the listener. He has the wonderful gift of instinctively sensing what is in the air. He has the ability to express this so clearly, logically, and openly that the listener feels that he has always agreed with what the Führer says. This is the real mystery of the magical effect of a Hitler speech. The Führer is neither a strictly intellectual nor a strictly emotional speaker. He speaks from both mind and heart, depending upon the situation. The essential characteristics of his speeches to the nation are: clarity of structure, relentlessly logical development of a series of thoughts, simplicity and comprehensibility, razor-sharp dialectic, a clear and infallible instinct for the masses and their feelings, a fascinating pathos that is used very sparingly, and the grace to call to the nation's souls in a way that the people will always answer.

Once, many years ago, when he was still far removed from power, the Führer spoke to a group consisting mainly of political opponents. He was met at first with icy rejection. In a two-hour long verbal boxing match with an obstinate audience he finally vanquished all reluctance and protest. Ultimately he was speaking into a bubbling sea of agreement, jubilation, and enthusiasm. As he closed, a voice from the highest row called out: "Hitler is a Columbus!"

This statement captures the essence of the man. He had succeeded in balancing an egg on its end. The times and the nations' longings were so confusing and mysterious; he had untangled them and had exposed the mysteries. He showed his audience in simple and clear ways just what the man on the street had long felt but had not had the courage to express. Hitler said what everyone else only thought and felt! And not only that: he had the civil courage to bring this to bear against the opposition of almost everyone, and to state with brazen logic the demands that arose from that time period and from the needs of the nation.

The Führer is the first in German history for whom language serves as a tool to make history. When he started, he had no other tools. He started out only with the force of his strong heart and the power of his pure word. With these he grasped the depth of the nation's soul. He did not speak like others. He could not be compared with them at all. It's not as though he didn't know the needs and concerns of the man on the street or did not speak of these things; but for him, these concerns were just brush-strokes on the terrible picture he painted of the collapse of Germany. He was not simply giving a performance, nor was he simply reporting like the rest. He raised the daily plight of individuals to a national level, giving lasting meaning to it. He appealed to the good instincts of the masses, not to the bad. His speech was like a magnet that drew anyone with iron in his veins to him.

For a while stupid and arrogant numskulls dismissed him as a 'political drummer.' They were making fools of themselves, and they didn't even know it. They so completely lacked the power of

The Führer opens the National Socialist Freedom Assembly in 1935 in the historical Nuremberg City Hall.

The Orator

Adolf Hitler

speech that they underestimated the power of speech in politics. They simply eyed power without realizing that Marxism had already wrested the power from them and that Marxism would give it up only if force were used. They formed conventicles when what they needed was a peoples' movement. They attempted coups when revolution was in the air. They had contempt for the masses because they did not want to become masters of the masses. The masses only yield to those who take them under their unrelenting command. They only obey someone who knows how to give orders. They instinctually know the difference between sincerity and empty words.

This is probably the most classic proof of the inner strength of the German nation, that it lends its ear to a man who stood up against state and economy, against press and public opinion, against what appeared to be reasonable and useful when all he offered was himself and his word. And this is also classic proof that the oratory genius of the Führer extends across all time, that his word alone shook the foundations of an entire period, rocked a seemingly solid state, and called forth a new time.

A historical oratory figure who effects such reactions must be able to use the spoken word in every situation. And so is it with the Führer. He speaks to workers just as clearly and confidently as to scientists. His word goes just as deeply into the hearts of the farmers as to the city folk. When he speaks to children he reaches their core, too. When he speaks to men, the lure of his voice brings forth their most secret emotions. His approach is historical philosophy, translated into the language of the people. He has a gift of being able to evoke long forgotten history, to bring it to the people who have never known anything about history, and to make his listeners feel they have known it all along.

His speeches are completely devoid of the arrogance that distinguishes the "educated."

Again and again his words revolve around the central ideas of the people and the national promotion of our race. He has a thousand ways to say these things. The listener never has the sense that something has already been said. Again and again, the same great, uplifting ideas for the rebirth of our nation are hammered into the masses with different words. He does not preach doctrine. He takes a fact, presents it as a thesis, and proceeds to back it up with an inexhaustible wealth of examples. These examples are not taken from a particular economic situation or from the life of a specific part of the population. If they were, the rest of the people would not be convinced. Rather, his examples come from the life of the entire population, and the whole population

Speaking to the youth

National Socialist Assembly in 1935

sees itself in them. They are so drawn by the strength of emotion that in the end even the most blindly enraged opponent will have to admit that, unlike the parliamentary jugglers, this orator believes what he says.

Everyday life comes alive here, holding everyone captive. The ravages of time are brought home using Weltanschauung as a tool, as well as humor and bitter irony. His humor is triumphant, the people cry with one eye and laugh with the other. He strikes a chord that sounds through the trials and plight of daily life.

An unmistakable indication as to whether a speech meets all these requirements is the fact that it reads well in addition to sounding good. The Führer's speeches are stylistic masterpieces whether improvised impromptu, whether using a few notes, or whether carefully recited at important international occasions. If you are not sitting very close to him, it is hard to tell if the Führer has written out his speech in full and is not using his notes or if he is speaking from a brief outline and just sounds like he has written out the complete speech. This is because both types of his speeches would be ready for publication. This picture of the Führer as orator would not be complete without mentioning the Führer as a towering shaper of ideas and a master of rhetorical discussion. The last time the public had an opportunity to get to know this side of him was during his falling out with the Social Democrats in the Reichstag in 1933. It was here that he responded to a crass and insolent lamentation by Wels, a member of the Reichstag at that time. The scene resembled a cat and mouse game. Marxism was pushed around from one end to the other. And when it wanted mercy, it got only destruction. With breathtaking precision the rhetorical whip hit its mark. With no manuscript, with no notes, the Führer had a great, long-desired reckoning with the social democratic parliamentary hard-liners, who suffered a death blow administered by the Führer.

How often had he driven them into the corner so long ago in his assemblies when they dared to confront him? Back then they were able to triumphantly spread insulting lies of his defeat in their newspapers the following day. Now, they stand face to face with his power with the entire nation watching, and disaster is upon them.

All of those judges and state's attorneys, using seemingly harmless, naive questions or crass and dull remarks, and wanting to lead Hitler, either as defendant or witness, onto thin ice had to sing the same song with this type of relentless oratorical offensive. A triumphant victory for the accused came out of the civil court process in 1924, which was to have legally purged the rebellion of the 8th and 9th of November, 1923. The Führer confronted the mountain of records, animosity, and lack of understanding with his open truthfulness and the penetrating effect of his gripping eloquence. And the Republic certainly regretfully wishes that the Leipzig Reichswehr trial in 1930 would not have taken place. This was supposed to defeat the Führer and his movement, but it actually became a springboard to his oratorical effectiveness that spread throughout the world. Today one shudders to remember the fact that a Jewish-Communist attorney had him stand as a witness in a Berlin court for nine uninterrupted hours against a firestorm of questions. And then we remember with proud satisfaction that this man faced Jewish Bolshevism and stubbornly upset its plans with words and ideas, unrelenting, until it lay overpowered on the ground.

We saw and experienced the Führer as a speaker at the National Socialist Party Assembly for Freedom in 1935. He spoke to the masses fifteen times over a period of seven days. Not once did he use the same expressions or present the same concepts. Again and again everything came across fresh, young, vital, and compelling. He spoke differently to the governors than to the SA and SS men, differently to the youth than to the women. Having revealed the most mysterious secrets of the arts in his great speech on culture, he turned to address the Wehrmacht and was understood by every single soldier right down to the last battalion. He is a bridge under which the life of the entire German nation moves and plays itself out. He has become a beacon of the word, making its thousand-fold presence known through his use of the godly blessing of language.

But the Führer is at his greatest as an orator when speaking to small groups of people. In these situations he turns continuously to each individual listener. This makes his discussions flow, and his conclusions follow immediately. He awakens the untiring interest of his listeners because they always feel he is telling them something new. He speaks with expert knowledge on any subject, astonishing everyone and impressing the experts. He is also able to quickly solve with universal solutions everyday problems that come up in the course of conversation.

Here, more intimately and in more detail than possible when speaking in public, the Führer gets to the core of issues and exposes the facts with relentless logic. Listening to him one on one just once is enough to grasp the greatness of his oratorical genius.

One can actually say of his addresses to the nation and to the world that his words find a circle of listeners as has never been seen in history. And they are words that ignite the heart and influence the shape of a new international epoch. Today there is hardly a person left in the entire developed world who has not heard the sound of his voice. Whether or not his words have been understood, the sound of them has reached the innermost part of peoples' hearts. Our nation can consider itself fortunate to know that the world is listening to a voice from here, a voice blessed to form words into thoughts and with these thoughts, to set things in motion. This man is one of those people with the courage to say "yes" and "no" without qualifying it in the next sentence with an "if" or a "but." Millions and millions of people in all countries of the world are subject to the most bitter pain, most devastating gloom and most horrible need. Hardly a star shines through the dark clouds shadowing Europe's sky. Nations are filled with hollow hope and are driven to verbalize these hopes, but lack the gift or grace to do so. But in Germany God has given one among untold millions the ability to put our suffering into words.

The Führer speaks to the German nation.

Taking a walk in the Obersalzberg mountains.

The Private Life of the Führer
by General Wilhelm Brückner

A man as caught up in political work as the Führer naturally must sacrifice his private life to it. And even when he tries to free himself from the pressures of official business, political problems follow him to the furthest reaches of the German homeland, whether it be a quiet little village in the dunes of the Baltic Sea or Haus Wachenfeld in Obersalzberg. It isn't only that he is besieged by telephone calls, telegrams, letters and files; he can never simply banish from his heart the constant political work or his concern about Germany. The Führer takes these cares to bed with him at night and awakes with them early in the morning. He is hounded by difficulties in foreign policy, by the requirements of a new labor battle, by difficulties arising in the arena of financial policies, by the need to secure nourishment for the German nation, by problems in educating the young, by questions of German culture, by decisions to be made in the course of re-establishing German military security. So it goes in motley succession; there is hardly a conversation that doesn't lead immediately to the most central political questions, not a single experience that doesn't remind him of important decisions to be made. Everything in Germany begins and ends with this man. And if he appears to rest completely secluded for a couple of days, he is actually preparing for great new decisions, for intensive new work and accomplishments. Even when he is flying, radio telegrams from his leaders of the Reich and his ministers still reach him.

And thus the private life of the Führer is completely consumed by his public office, by his work for Germany. If one wants to speak of a private life, one can only really say that it consists of moving political work from the rooms of the chancellery to less official rooms.

Despite all of this, he manages to find time to deal with all matters of art and science. He finds the greatest and most delightful relaxation from his grueling daily routine in music, listening to opera or the symphony. Only then is he set completely free from the pressing questions of the day, and many a creative idea was born while he was engrossed in the powerful richness of sound.

Even in the rooms of his official residence in the chancellery, the Führer has leading German artists as his guests from time to time. They expose him to the best creative work of our time. After their artistic presentations the discussions of music, drama, poetry, fiction, architecture, and philosophy frequently stretch long into the night. No one could leave the house after such an evening without feeling intellectually stimulated.

In addition to music, theater and architecture, the Führer is particularly attracted to film, since it is the newest branch of artistic creation. A movie projector in the great hall of the chancellery of the Reich makes it possible to view the on-going production of Germany and the world in between dealing with pressing questions of the day. The Führer's knowledge has provided much new stimulus even to those in the film industry.

He frequently invites visitors who have appeared before him for official meetings to share the noon meal with him, so that he can discuss in more detail any questions that occurred to him during the official presentation. Thus people from various fields of work and interests – officers and scientists, men of business and the arts, high party leaders and

A neighbor in Obersalzberg greets the Führer.

He is allowed to peer through the telescope.

Prime Minister Göring with the Führer in Obersalzberg.

A field comrade visits with the Führer.

Haus Wachenfeld in Obersalzberg near Berchtesgaden.

An encounter in Obersalzberg.

old comrades-in-arms from the war and the early days of the movement — frequently come together at the Führer's table and receive new knowledge and intellectual stimulation, not just from him but also in discussions among themselves.

The Führer likes to use the weekend to personally gauge the mood of the nation, and to form a picture of the progress of reconstruction work, without officially scheduled visits. He drives through the German Gaue (districts) in his cherished wartime automobile, and almost every location stirs some memory from the time of the struggle for power. Over and over on these trips his entourage relives the profound experience of seeing the nation's enormous love for the Führer come surging forth.

There are some places in Germany which the Führer especially favors for short rests. Above all there is the house in Obersalzberg, well known to all Germans, which is so closely connected with the history of the movement. There are a couple of places hidden in the dunes of the Baltic Sea and the North Sea which the Führer likes to seek out for a short holiday or to hold especially important meetings. Walks through a beech forest at sunset on the seashore often provide rest and relaxation while helping reach important political decisions at the same time. Children approach him without fear on these walks, offer him their hands, chat with him, sharing with him all the little experiences that are so important to them. Sometimes the Führer interrupts the most important conversations so he can abandon himself for a few minutes completely to the joys and the sorrows of such a child. In the larger maritime cities the navy gathers around the Führer to enliven a brief, casual evening with stories of the war, reports from U-boat cruises and of the battles at Skagerrak. It is the same in small

Taking a walk in the mountains.

A day of rest. The Führer and little Helga Goebbels.

A simple stew, even for the Chancellor of the German Reich.

Good news.

A Hitler Youth hands the Führer a letter from his sick mother.

A little one visits the Führer in Obersalzberg.

garrisons and in the countryside, where the Führer himself often tells exciting and impressive stories of his war experiences on the western front.

During his travels, he frequently breaks for a quick picnic at particularly charming scenic points, whether on a radiant summer Sunday or on a warm and beautiful moonlit night. And often berry pickers or people out gathering wood suddenly draw near and pause, surprised to see that it is the Führer here on a forest glade, peeling an apple or eating a couple of pieces of bread. Then he beckons the hesitant onlookers to draw near, inviting them to partake of his meal.

Many people wonder why the Führer selected Obersalzberg as his home. But anyone who has stood there high up on the mountainside understands that there is hardly a town in all of Germany from which one has such a wide and unobstructed view of the world's beauty, despite the proximity of the surrounding mountains. To the north, nestled at the foot of the Gaisberg, lies the old cathedral city of Salzburg.

When a *foehn* wind blows, clearing the air, you can see the castle and the little town with the naked eye. Even without the *foehn*, with binoculars you can see all the details of the buildings. To the left of Obersalzberg looms the massive peak of the Untersberg, providing an ever-changing experience with different, enchanting colors. Still further to the left, your eyes wander over to Watzmann Mountain and to the other large mountains surrounding it archlike, ending up behind Obersalzberg in the high Göll.

No day here is like any other. Sometimes fog brews in the morning, leading to a desperate battle against the sun located higher in the sky, until the fog is overcome and rises from the valleys to hover, near midday, as soft white clouds against an azure blue sky. At other times, the day begins with radiant sun light, and the observer sees everything clearly and distinctly, down to the last detail. The foehn comes down warm from the heights and fills the valleys with a soft, nostalgic atmosphere. Then rain and snowstorms whip the mountains, and the wind blusters around the simple little country house.

In a G'schwandner alpine pasture near Garmisch.

The Führer during summer vacation in front of the Bruckerlehen near Berchtesgaden where Dietrich Eckart lived for some time in 1923.

Evening in Obersalzberg.

Four strapping brothers.

A mother's pride and joy.

"Here, my Führer, is my grandchild."

Here, surrounded by this magnificent nature, which is an allegory of human events, the Führer prepares his great speeches, often giving not just Germany but international politics new impetus or direction. This is where the crucial meetings take place, before great laws – calculated to influence centuries to come – take on their final form.

A German-American from the Steuben Society understood the significance of this little country house when he became acquainted with it on a visit to his old homeland. He later said: "We Germans from America do not know the new Germany. We know only the old Germany, and we have seen it again with new eyes as we visited the palaces and castles of earlier times. Now we have become acquainted with this house and have experienced it as an obvious example of the contrast between the Germany created by Adolf Hitler and the old one. We now also know the inexhaustible fount from which he draws the substance for his speeches."

And it is true that here, far from the confusing hustle and bustle of everyday life, the searching mind, guided by the endless spectacle of the landscape, finds the right paths for the nation and the fatherland. But the Führer is not able to enjoy the wondrous beauty of nature like someone on vacation who has left all his business behind. Even as he arrives in Obersalzberg, he encounters an imposing number of letters and files, telegrams and telephone messages, and new piles of work arrive with every postal delivery. Ministers and leaders of the Reich call him almost every day to get his view on important and urgent matters. Often they themselves make the journey to Berchtesgaden to talk to the Führer during his short period of

The Führer in front of his country house in Obersalzberg.

rest. Party questions that have been deferred because of important political decisions in Berlin are settled here, and many books – belles lettres as well as political literature, both foreign and domestic – which languished uselessly in the chancellery of the Reich, are read thoroughly here by the Führer in peace and quiet. This is when the light in his room burns until late at night. Often, long after his entourage has retired, magnificently deep peace reigns, and the Führer reads – these are his happiest hours. The next morning, the long-distance exchange begins again with dozens of person-to-person telephone calls, the files lie waiting, the mail piles up. Yes, the sad truth is this: When the Führer is in Obersalzberg "for rest and relaxation," the post office and telephone company in Berchtesgaden are working at their peak. And everyone surrounding the Führer puts in a good measure of work, because it is here that ideas come easily and decisions ripen quickly.

Before eating a common breakfast, the Führer has already read the newspapers, which he goes through himself instead of having someone prepare excerpts for him. Then his adjutants, his press chief, and the other men in his entourage report briefly on what is on the day's agenda. Then they eat breakfast, and immediately afterwards the scheduled visitors, leaders of the Reich, ministers, close staff members and party members arrive. In the meantime, the mail is prepared and reported on to the Führer, who outlines brief responses or dictates immediate responses himself. And so the morning passes quickly.

The old guard is always cheerfully received as guests in Obersalzberg: party comrades Göring and Dr. Goebbels, Reich's Treasury Minister Schwarz, Minister Adolf Wagner, the Reich's Minister of War and many others.

Usually the busy morning is followed by a short or long midday walk, or by a trip into the surrounding countryside. In both summer and winter, the Führer especially likes to hike to "Göll Häusl" where Dietrich Eckart lived until death tore him from the Führer's side.

The Führer is just as happy to travel over to Königsee, an unparalleled jewel of the German mountain landscape, where the sheer drop of the Watzmann and the idyllic Bartholomew offer unforgettable splendor.

If there is not enough time for longer walks, and if work must continue immediately after the midday meal, then at coffee time there is usually some time to go to the little mountain inn on Hochlenzer or to pay a visit to Prime Minister Göring's house if the master of the house is at home, in which case Göring may invite the Führer to an archery match, a sport at which he is a master.

Often, however, the Führer has just a few minutes to spare during the day, which he spends in the garden of the house with his German shepherds, who cling to him with idolatrous love. In winter, Adolf Hitler pensively watches the birds in their various feeding areas as they help themselves to what he has scattered for them in the morning.

At Obersee, a lake near Berchtesgaden

Thus the daily schedule changes from day to day. Only one event is absolutely fixed. Every day at midday, hundreds and thousands of comrades gather below on the roadway to see the Führer. The Führer, who well knows that they have all come to Berchtesgaden not just to see him, but to express the love of the entire nation, allows nothing to stop him from fulfilling their fondest wish. It is always a heart stirring image to experience the jubilation which breaks outs when the Führer enters their midst. Blue collar and white collar workers alike gather here from all over Germany, and it is always like a pilgrimage. All of them, large and small, march past the Führer. Their eyes sparkle, their hands are raised in salute, and many of them have tears of profound emotion in their eyes. Cheers ring out from the ranks of the marchers as they announce their affiliation with individual Teutonic tribes, "from Upper Silesia," "from East Prussia," "from Schleswig," "from Oldenburg," "from Saxony," "from Hamburg" and so on. Young members of the Hitler Youth and the League of German Girls are not held back by barricades. As swift as hares, they rush to the Führer, presenting him with carefully prepared little bouquets of flowers. They are happy if the Führer talks to them and even more thrilled if he invites some of them to have lunch or coffee with him.

All of his guests and his staff sit happily together at mealtimes, and hearty laughter often rings out through the room. These brief minutes pass in peaceful relaxation. Architects and artists visit frequently, presenting their new plans to the Führer. He is pleased by everything dealing with cultural reconstruction and engages in long discussions of the plans. The Führer also pays strict attention to the plans and photographs of Dr. Todt, the General Inspector for the Reich's autobahns. And the Führer's old comrades-in-arms from the great war are always welcome guests in Obersalzberg.

But even though there is no end to the work in Obersalzberg, short, vigorous walks provide the Führer with new buoyancy. It is all the same to him whether the hot summer sun is blazing from the sky or crunchy snow covers the mountains, whether rain beats down or fog conceals all. The Führer walks very briskly so these walks are not always pure pleasure for the Führer's entourage, men who have gone to the big city and forgotten real mountain climbing. It is often difficult even for people who are in good shape to keep pace with him, and his adjutants sometimes have trouble matching his speed. The Führer strides along quickly and effortlessly, while they have already begun to huff and puff.

These are only brief days of relaxation, and more often than not, unexpected events cut them even shorter. But one thing is sure: nowhere will the Führer find a life that is so tailored to his nature as the life he lives in the few days that he is able to spend here on the mountain.

Just as the mountains remain eternal amidst the changes of thousands of years, so too will the work the Führer has begun here live on for millennia, through his nation.

During summer vacation in Obersalzberg.

New Year's Day reception for the Diplomatic Corps 1934.

The Führer as Statesman
by Dr. Joseph Goebbels

All human greatness has its source in the blood. Greatness is guided by instinct, and intuition is its great blessing. The participation of the intellect in works of true genius is always limited; the intellect has more to do with ferreting out the direction and meaning of these works and revealing them to later observers. These laws apply particularly to the arts, the highest and most noble activity of man, which bring him closer to his divine source. In the same way the arts have value and meaning in the field of politics. It is no coincidence that we refer to "the art of statesmanship." Statesmanship is truly an art because it has all the characteristics of artistic creativity. The sculptor uses chisel and hammer on untreated stone to blow divine breath into it, and raw marble becomes artistic form. The painter uses the medium of color to recreate what nature has so nobly provided, and to re-create it again, as it were. The writer strings sentence together using language (in itself formless) to make a poem, a drama, or an epic work, in which he recasts human passions and the good and evil within these passions. The statesman has the raw material of the masses at his disposal. With the power of his words and works, he molds them to a living, breathing, national entity. His great, inspired projects give the public a national goal. Everyone draws equally from the brilliant ideology which originates as inspiration. And the true artist always considers himself to be only its instrument. Each of these areas has its necessary craftsmen who exist within the limitations of their tasks and duties. They learn their craft industriously and conscientiously. Those who are among the better craftsmen acquire valuable and extensive knowledge of their specialty, and they understand what is required of them. But they have a profession, not a calling. These are talented craftsmen. The true artist, however, is a genius.

This is the difference between talent and genius: talent draws on experience, on knowledge, perhaps from an imaginative intellect. Genius, however, draws on grace. Genius is challenged to a higher task, thus fulfilling the law according to which it is called.

Geniuses overthrow worlds and build new worlds. Geniuses are the great signpost for all nations. Whole eras orient themselves according to the geniuses of the time. Geniuses set the course of history.

There is a saying that inside every man is a child. This is especially valid for the genius because the actions and works of a genius are characterized by childlike spontaneity. A genius approaches things with the same confident instinct of a child.

A brilliant statesman dares the impossible to make possible what is possible. His real strength is in simplifying problems that seem insoluble. Before those of average intelligence have even identified or recognized a problem, the great Führer is already solving it.

The most urgent problem that the Germans needed to solve after the war was to take the conglomerate of states, parties, organizations, and individuals and form a nation that would be united in its thinking, its feelings, and its action. This problem did not originate with the war; but ultimately the fact that it remained unsolved is the reason we lost the war. For many centuries Germany was excluded from being an actor in world politics because of its inner disunity. We Germans were at odds with each other about religious, economic, and social issues. These internal battles were terrible and claimed large numbers of victims, while other nations, recognizing their political destiny earlier, took possession of the globe.

The war made it clear that this situation was untenable. But the Germans did not learn from this terrible lesson. Instead we did exactly the opposite of what history demanded of us. Unprecedented divisiveness was observed at a time when we were most dependent on our internal unity.

In the years after the war Germany sometimes gave the impression that it was in the process of leaving behind the sphere of large-scale interaction with world powers to withdraw into provincial isolation. There were none of the prerequisites for standardization of national thought. One can even say that the so-called Weimar Constitution represented perpetuation of internal conflict and that it was the parliamentary parties who were the greedy beneficiaries. The state shirked this responsibility because its vigilance was directed inward rather than outward. Its goal was to keep and conserve what little remained of our internal freedom and outer sovereignty.

The first and most difficult test for the brilliant statesman appearing on the scene at this time was to recognize that a struggle within the state itself to reestablish Germany as a world power was

Visit in the chancellery of the Reich (Prime Minister Gömbös)

pointless from the very beginning. Thus it was useless even to try because, by signing the Treaty of Versailles, the state had given up once and for all its status as a world power.

Furthermore, it zealously enforced the treaty. Every stirring of nationalism was considered an attack on the state itself and was punished.

And so at that time, a true statesman could be found only outside the state, not from within the parties and not from within the state. The state had to fall first to then make possible moral, social, and economic restoration of the German nation; and with restoration, the consolidation of a true state as befitting the real nature of the nation. It was necessary in this struggle against the state to form a state within a state, to be a testing ground for

A historical meeting. Eden and Simon with the Führer.

The Reich's Cabinet at the announcement of national defense legislation.

After the reception for the diplomats on New Year's Day 1936.

The Führer and Foreign Minister von Neurath.

Adolf Hitler's meeting with Mussolini in Venice 1934.

In the chancellery of the Reich: the Führer and his Chief of Staff Lutze.

the practical and organizational laws that would later be the fundamental laws of the new state. It was not enough to counter Weimar theory with a new theory, even if well conceived and well meant. A group of men would have to rally around the new theory – men who would give this theory life, color, and a real existence. The basic idea was that there would have to be a new, opposing state within the Weimar Republic. People would have to support this new state, and they would become the new nation which would emerge from the old Weimar Republic. The process of developing a new German nation could be successfully begun only in accordance with these principles.

And it is here that the Führer's work as a statesman began.

But before he could begin, there were some basic decisions to make. These were to become the actual source of his political actions. Even when he was still an unknown private first-class in the World War, speaking as an education officer to Bavarian garrisons, the Führer made numerous decisions. These decisions suggest that he was acting with absolute confidence and with the superior instinct of a statesman-genius. Most particularly, it is the fact that almost no one understood his actions – a fact that was later the actual reason for his fabulous, fantastic rise – which confirms the absolute correctness of the philosophy taking shape in his mind. It would have been easy for him to join one of the existing parties where he would have had a quiet, secure life and prospects of advancement. He could have quieted his tortured conscience with the argument that one had to save what could be saved and that it was therefore necessary to choose the lesser evil. He did not do this. He

The Reich's Chancellor at the New Year's reception talking to the French ambassador François-Poncet.

New Year's reception 1935. The Führer speaks with the doyen of the diplomatic corps.

The Führer and Polish Foreigner Minister Colonel Beck.

Reich's Press Chief Dr. Dietrich presenting press reports to the Führer.

In the Chancellery of the Reich.

Soldiers from the English front with the Führer.

did not do it because none of the existing parties could guarantee a solution to the disunity within Germany. None of the existing parties even had a chance. But he knew that without unifying the Germans, a statesmanlike approach to the national German problem – although there was a solution – would be impossible from the very beginning. Here one can already see the instincts of a gifted man who would prefer to choose what seemed to be a hopeless, desperate struggle against state, money, press, and parties rather than burdening the very beginning of his work with a compromise.

It was fashionable at the time to support the state. There were two separate camps. One identified itself with the state, and the other believed it could and should reform the state from the inside. The Führer belonged to neither camp because he knew that the state was flawed at its very foundation. And so he knew the state could not be reorganized, but rather that it would have to be eliminated to make it possible to form a true state. Later there were people and parties who went against the Weimar system when they recognized, or pretended to recognize, the impossibility of internal reform. But they were already burdened with the onus of having made peace with the Weimar democracy, even if temporarily.

The Führer was the only one who could point to the fact that at no time had he entered into an agreement with the parliamentary regime. Thus it appeared that he alone was predestined to give it the final blow in its last hour.

At that time, parties and individuals did not speak to the people as a nation. They only addressed separate groups within the nation. The worker parties spoke to the workers, the conservative parties spoke to the middle class, the religious parties to their adherents, and the farmers' parties to the farmers. At the early meetings of the National Socialist German Workers' Party in Munich, where the Führer spoke to an audience of barely one hundred, it may have seemed grotesque to the casual observer that it was always the nation as a whole whom he addressed. This party did not speak to the educated population alone or to the proletariat alone. Hitler had the courage to say unpopular things, and he spurned cheap flattery that would have bought him the applause of the masses. Today one has to look back on these origins of the National Socialist movement and to the true leadership of Adolf Hitler to understand the miracle of the statesmanlike approach founded in these origins. For it was not the times that had changed the Führer, but the Führer who changed the times. What seemed a paradox then has long since become self-evident. But it did not become self-evident on its own; no, it needed a clear and uncompromising decision by a man and a dogged and relentless struggle until it had achieved its goal.

Memorial Day 1934. The ceremony in the Berliner Staatsoper.

It would have been easy then to suggest social reforms which could have been exaggerated more and more the further the Führer and his movement were from actual fulfillment of promises made. It's true that for the first few years it would probably have been more convenient to win supporters this way. The Führer did not do this. He gave his movement an ideological platform that became, as it were, the fundamental foundation of his party and state. The most essential characteristic of this ideology was the connection between the nation and socialist principles. These two driving forces, engaged in a bitter struggle at the time, were thus brought together on a higher plane and yet in a simple manner that the man on the street could understand. The fact that nothing needed to be changed when the National Socialist movement came to power – not the program nor the ideology, not the flag nor the name, is proof of how farsighted and statesmanlike the foundation for the National Socialist framework was in the very early days of the party. The Führer trained the party not to compromise. The party combined absolute implacability regarding its principles with the highest flexibility regarding its methods and actions. From the very first day until the party destroyed it, the party was engaged in a life and death struggle with parliamentarianism. The party did not retreat before the terror of the Marxist parties with their feeble and cowardly clichés, but used brute force against brute force. Even though the party's daring first surprise putsch on November 8 and 9, 1923 was unsuccessful, later historians will need to examine not only what was achieved, but also what was prevented. There is no question that their judgment will fully justify the Führer's actions. And how did conservative politicians act during the days of the Republic, after lost coups? Either they fled abroad or they were not there. But the Führer was different! He stood at the front of his troops. He was the first amongst the accused; he did not take the easy way out although the courts and government offered him opportunities; he did not allow himself to be persuaded, but openly admitted that he had wanted to overthrow the state and that he would do it again and again, whenever he saw an opportunity. He took the most dangerous and most destructive path, and his actions saved the movement and his work. At the trial at People's Court in Munich he conducted himself in an utmost statesmanlike way, illustrating all the elements of the highest order of political action. He paired boldness with logic, and honesty with courage. He showed contempt for danger when the stakes were the highest. This was the last game of chance. There was everything to win because everything had been wagered. Self-defense against the non-state of Versailles and Weimar was heightened to a higher moral principle and it carried away hundreds of thousands of people in a flood of enthusiastic admiration – people who until then had only dreamed of it, yearned for it. The Führer cannot be held responsible for the road the party took while he was incarcerated. He so clearly recognized the tasks of the statesman that awaited him after his release that his party did not merge with others, which might have made things easier for him. Rather he founded the old movement anew according to the principles established in beginning. Thus began the hard struggle, replete with victims and sacrifice, to rebuild the prestige of the party. For years it seemed hopeless. At the time the NSDAP was not even considered worthy of the hatred of its opponents. Although barely visible externally, it developed internally into a fertile, organic process of gradual reconstruction of the movement and its separate organizations. If a statesman is judged by how he gathers minds, character, and personalities around himself and his work, the Führer need not fear being compared to others. Few eras in history could boast

The Führer in front of the Kaiserplatz in Goslar at the harvest thanksgiving celebration, 1934.

the wealth of expertise we have experienced in our time. Today they are visible. But it was harder to find them among the masses of supporters, to instinctively recognize their talents, and to place them in the movement's struggle – and later within the state – according to their capabilities.

Whereas in 1928 there were only twelve delegates of the National Socialist movement in parliament, this number increased nearly tenfold within two years. The party stepped into the limelight and found itself facing its most difficult test. It could let itself be cast aside with a few minor minister posts like the other parties and participate in the regime, or it could continue the struggle to the end, no matter what the outcome, under the motto "all or nothing."

Again the Führer's instinct as a statesman enabled him to make the right decision. The struggle continued, and the party found its voice during the Reich's defense trial before the Federal Court in Leipzig when the Führer himself proclaimed his understanding of the principle of legality. It is doubtful whether anyone in the regime foresaw at the beginning of this trial that, by the time it was over, a democratic Berlin newspaper would write with resignation that the real winner was Adolf Hitler. In addition they wrote that the highest German court had given him an opportunity to corroborate under oath – in front of the whole world – his understanding of the principle of legality. Up to this point they had not allowed this because of their past experiences with him, and now he could forever point to his understanding of this principle in his struggle against the republic. This was a turning point, and this is what distinguished the Führer from his opponents. With his statesman's vision he had seen the possibilities of this trial from the beginning, whereas his opponents had not seen its significance until the end. It was absolutely clear to him that he had to assert the principle of legality against the extremists in his own party. He also knew that it was necessary to do so if the movement were to strike its decisive blow.

The next goal was to gradually crack open and systematically weaken the conservative parties. Two years later, unflagging efforts in this respect caused the downfall of the Brüning cabinet. The feigned tolerance for the Papen government led to the thirteenth of August 1932. Here again, a great hour dawned for a true statesman. Here again it was a matter of either being satisfied with half or wanting it all. Any politician would have gone for the former, and German history has dozens of

Foreign military attaches at the party congress in Nuremberg.

examples to prove it. But the Führer, a true statesman, opted for the latter. He lost two million votes in the November 1932 election for this great, bold decision. With an unprecedented concentration of force, he undertook a final assault against the regime in the Lippe elections early in January of 1933. Two weeks later he was in power.

The first symbol of building the foundation was the alliance between Hindenburg and Hitler. Here tradition and revolution joined hands. The statesman-genius of the Führer produced the miracle of a virtually bloodless revolution while simultaneously reconciling with true traditional values.

Here we see the value of confidently adhering to his instinct regarding his Weltanschauung – the instinct of a man who acts responsibly and who effortlessly follows his conscience. They scorned radical rhetoric and a magnificent transformation

A meeting of Reich's governors in the chancellery of the Reich under the Führer's chairmanship.

The Führer receiving a delegation from the Japanese Navy, 1934.

took place: one world was felled and a new world was built.

This is the miracle of German unity. The Führer made traditional values part of the state on March 21, 1933. He made the German workers part of the state on May 1, 1933. An almost inevitable result of this re-fusion of the nation was the occupation of the union's buildings at the one time when it was possible, and indeed, at the tactically correct moment. Likewise, the implementation of a four-year plan to solve Germany's most urgent problems was a farsighted and thorough blueprint requiring time to work peacefully and calmly. Next, the Führer considered the huge number of urgent problems facing his public policies. He earmarked a just a few very important problems and solved them using the greatest and best resources. Here again he was always too perfect a statesman. Never was there a great revolutionary less hysterical or less rash than he. Never had a politician making history worked so clearly and purposefully, or so calmly and quietly. And never in history had such a miracle taken place while under such pressure from abroad!

The Führer's decision for Germany to leave the League of Nations was daring and significant. Where others were more timid and filled with hopelessness, Hitler was clear and decisive. This decision was necessary even if risky. Ever the statesman, Hitler arranged for the people themselves to vote on this monumental issue that first year. Ever the statesman, he chose the most critical moment to proclaim Germany's freedom to arm itself again and to present this to the world as an irreversible fact. He knew that the time was right, and so he acted. This is proof of true vocation. In this case when a man acts, he acts under a higher law. In this case he is acting not on intellect but on the instinct that is in his blood.

A German nation finally able to protect itself

*Labor Day, May 1, 1934. Youth rally in the Berliner Lustgarten.
The Führer departs after his great speech to the young people.*

again, a German nation with a straightforward agreement with England to have a German navy adequate for the population, a German nation that has re-entered the circle of other nations as a world power, a German nation more and more admired, or at least envied by the whole world, and a German nation becoming ever more visible as an important element of world peace – all this from a seven-member party in Munich brought to great power by a statesman. This development was guided by a number of decisions, all of which illustrate a fabulous and fantastic rise that future historians are sure to praise as the greatest political miracle of the twentieth century.

It is here that clear thinking came together with purposeful action. It is here that political instinct, unspoiled through and through, accomplished its task. It is here that an unerring instinct was at play, that of knowing when something is possible and when something is not possible. It is here that instinct brought about miracles because there was belief in miracles.

The German people today are not the same as the German people of ten years ago. The nation owes its strength and its belief to the confident, unswerving leadership of a true statesman – a statesman who knows what he wants, and wants what he knows. He belongs to the few chosen people in history. He is great enough to be simple and simple enough to be great!

At Tempelhof Field on May 1.

The Führer lays the foundation for a community center in the Adolf Hitler Koog.

The Führer and the German Worker
By Dr. Robert Ley

The change that has taken place in the German nation since it was taken over by National Socialism is most clearly seen in the attitude of the worker toward the new German state and in the value placed on the worker and his work.

The working class arose at a time when liberalism began to rule Europe's world of thought. Liberalism has always depicted work as something disagreeable, even dishonorable. The highest ideal of liberalism was to live from the work of others. No longer was the most desirable goal that of helping to build the nation's future and to experience the joy inherent in this activity. Instead, the goal was to put this disagreeable condition known as work behind oneself, to live on annuities and dividends, and at most to derive an income from real estate or commerce. Obviously, when this is the prevailing attitude toward life, work is devalued and the scale becomes something like this: at the top end are the do-nothing blasé, next come those who work in finance or trade, then come the professionals and, at the very bottom of the scale, manual laborers.

By God, physical work was the dirtiest and most debasing thing that could happen to a human being. Anyone unfortunate enough to have to earn a living with his hands was completely unsuitable for and excluded from "good company." The fact that the worker, toiling day after day by the sweat of his brow, feels inferior is proof that this liberal Weltanschauung has poisoned the positive national attitude. Why else would a father scrape his pennies together to enable his son to become "something better"-a craftsman perhaps.

With workers in Siemensstadt

And then spend every penny of his meager wage to send his son to high school or at least to middle school if the boy has trouble learning Latin and mathematics. And the father does not say that he does this so his son will have an easier life; so he can face life better prepared; so he will have a better life than his father. No, he says explicitly that he is doing this so that his son can climb the social ladder.

Is it possible to understand the insanity of this kind of thinking-this insanity that was indeed systematically encouraged by Marxism? Marxism did its best to deepen the feeling of inferiority that this liberal arrogance had instilled in the German worker, and to forever infuse the German worker with a feeling of being "disinherited" or nothing but a "proletarian," and to believe that he should hate those who are "better."

The forces of Liberalism and Marxism, growing from the same seed and separated into castes by class hatred, committed this cursed crime!

Seduced by Marxism, the worker believed that he could improve his situation by refusing to work. The liberals dulled people's minds so that many of the "educated" went hungry rather then engaging in manual labor. The good German saying, "Work does not dishonor" was turned around: "Work dishonors!" The propertied classes saw in the worker a dirty slave. The worker took revenge by considering everyone who offered employment a bloodsucker and a drone, and he began to treat them accordingly. Neither side noticed that their views and actions would quickly destroy the nation that, for better or worse, they were both part of. As far as the International Labor Association was concerned, neither the gold, the green nor the red had room for a fatherland named Germany.

And it is here that Adolf Hitler's extraordinary work began. He realized that it was not a question of the haves and have-nots, not a question of employers and employees. He realized that Marxism could not be stamped out without stamping out this arrogant and reactionary liberalism. He introduced the people to a system of values that was as new as it was ancient.

People stopped to listen to Hitler's brief, clear words. At first only a few were moved by what he had to say, then more and more were moved, and finally everyone saw that for the last century they had been stumbling around in the deepest, most terrible darkness. Their eyes were opened to a new, brilliant realization. In the light of this realization, everything that had been so hostile, everything that had seemed to be an unresolvable conflict, all this deathly animosity dissolved into

Young workers visiting the Führer in the chancellery on May 1, 1934

At a Blohm & Voss shipyard, 1934.

National Socialist Party rally in 1935. The Führer and Dr. Ley with large groups of workers.

The Führer at the Automobile Expo in Berlin, 1935.

Laying the cornerstone of a new Reichsbank, May 5, 1934.

nothing. The Führer teaches us: you are nothing, your nation is everything. When you work, you work for your nation. It is an honor to work. All work is the same. The work of a managing director is no more valuable than the work of a street sweeper. It does not matter what kind of work is done, only that it is done. Those who do not work lose honor in the national community. Work does not dishonor; it ennobles the worker. It makes no difference if it is intellectual work or manual work. The only dishonor is to be a drone with contempt for those who work.

And these words were more than theory. German workers in 1933-seduced by Marxism and reactionary, dull-minded liberals-may have been skeptical and may have believed that the Weltanschauung of National Socialism was not quite serious. But this changed within a very short time, and today the German worker is a staunch follower of the Führer-the Führer who freed him from his proletarian existence, who returned to him the honor and work which liberalism and Marxism had taken from him, who finally gave him that which, in his heart of hearts, he had always struggled for: to be respected by others; to have the same value placed on all work; and to have workers differentiated from each other only by their effort and efficiency.

Once this became clear, the German workers enthusiastically followed the Führer and stood shoulder to shoulder next to the first worker of the Reich. Even the liberals among the propertied classes changed their ideas and learned the National Socialist way of thinking. By the third year of the National Socialist Reich, this new work ethic was outwardly evident in the final stabilization of the

Visiting the Bavarian Motor Works.

A Mercedez-Benz race car built upon the Führer's suggestion.

This is how a statesman moves among workers.

Visiting industry in Rhein-Westphalia.

Visit to a factory. A representative of the work force greets the Führer.

Labor Corps working to reclaim land from the sea.

German Labor Front as an organization which included all working Germans, from managing directors to apprentices. From this day forward only Germans work in Germany and only German businesses exist there. The past is definitively dead. The nobility of work rules in Germany.

This could only happen because each and every German learned a new way of thinking and began to look at the world in a new way, namely from the viewpoint of National Socialism. The Führer once said, "He who wants to be a true socialist must himself have experienced deprivation." The German working masses know that the Führer himself was a manual laborer for many years. They know that he has experienced first-hand how hard it is to work from morning until night in the sun, rain and wind, in cold and heat. The ideas that propel National Socialism could only come from this kind of a man. He spoke from experience when he talked about the fact that it was an honor to work, and the masses knew exactly what he meant. This is the mysterious bond between the German worker and the Führer. The Führer freed the worker from a slave-like existence, giving back to him the honor of a free man. So today National Socialism rests firmly and securely within the working class. And so it is only natural that on the First of May, a national holiday for the German nation, delegations of German workers come to see the Führer. And it is natural that these delegations are made up of the entire spectrum of the German work force: those who work with their heads as well as those who work with their hands.

They come from all regions of the Reich, invited by the nation. They come by airplane and by express train, and they stay in the big hotels in this cosmopolitan city. They bring the Führer hand-crafted gifts, greetings from their comrades, and the assurance of their loyalty, love, and trust. They stand face to face with him before accompanying him to the colossal rallies on German Labor Day.

understood only if seen from this point of view. In earlier days, no one cared what the workstations looked like or where the German worker labored for the nation. Today, the Office of "Work Beautification" makes certain that the German worker has a work place worthy of him and that he is not stuck in a broom closet somewhere. The "Strength through Joy" movement offers today's

International Automobile Expo, Berlin 1935: the protector of the automobile industry.

Perhaps there is still room for improvement. It may be that here and there people make mistakes, and difficulties arise due to scarcity and lack of judgment. Self-interest and meanness are still around in some places. It may be that some people are still not willing to accept the new gospel: working for honor. But these are nothing but insignificant and marginal phenomena. The workers do not care about these exceptions because the word is out, and the word must be allowed to spread, the word that tells of the nobility of work. The activities of the German Labor Front can be

German workers vacations and opportunities for relaxation. Today's workers can travel to the mountains or to the seaside. Today's workers can hike, often for the very first time, through this beautiful fatherland. Today's workers can take German ships to the magical southern seas and countries or to the sublime beauty of the north.
Just like any other comrade, the workers enjoy the great achievements of German theater and German music, the best German orchestras, the best German opera, theater and film performances. They listen to the radio for entertainment, and

they can pursue any number of sports. But it is not hedonism, diversion, or satisfying physical desires that fulfills them. They derive true and noble pleasure from their physical being, from nature and from culture. The harder one works, the more joyful he should be, and this joy makes him even more valuable to his nation. The nation is no longer paralyzed by the scourge of unemployment. Millions have found work again and those who are still on the sideline are protected by the whole nation. Labor representatives make certain that workers' right to life and honor remains untouched. Managers are responsible for the well-being of their teams just as workers and managers together are responsible for the success of the company in which both work. This is a basic difference between National Socialism and the past: in the past you had many chairmen and many people under each chairman – chairmen of supervisory boards, administrative boards, parties, unions and management associations, social aid organizations, and strike committees. Today we have one Führer for the whole nation. Leaders stand behind him, each with a special field or group of people. Before, "one man sat higher than the other," but they all just sat. They had no goal and no path to follow. In contrast, today they have direction, path, and goal; they have set out marching behind one leader.

Even the language, the words themselves, express the great difference between two eras.

Each and every German knows that there is only one man to thank for all this, Adolf Hitler-who created National Socialism, who put the common good above selfishness, who did away with class struggle between upper and lower, between right and left – when he proclaimed that there is honor in work and in service to the nation. The existence of the National Socialist Labor Corps, where every German must work at manual labor for the benefit of the nation before he can work for his own benefit, guarantees that the lessons that enable the German worker to carry the weight of the state will never be lost.

The Führer exorcised from Germany arrogance contempt, envy, and hatred of work and property. He gave the people a sense of honor and pride that they were workers. They would therefore feel that it is their duty to serve the whole nation. Today's German worker is happy to be a free man in a free country. Today's German worker is the best worker in the world. Future centuries will envy him. Today's German worker, from the depths of his heart, thanks the Führer, the man who has given him all of this.

This is how German farmers greet their Führer, Adolf Hitler, Bückeberg 1935.

At the Berlin Philharmonic Hall. The Führer at a concert of the Philharmonic Orchestra under the direction of conductor Wilhelm Furtwängler.

The Führer and the Arts
by Dr. Joseph Goebbels

Art is the most noble activity of the human soul and imagination. Art is a way of giving form to feeling. An artist expresses what he holds in his heart. Intense feelings demand intense forms of expression. An artist can give voice to his inner daemon. Artists express in words, sounds, stone, and marble that which the masses sometimes feel only as a dark, dull yearning. Throughout history art has uplifted men and touched them to the quick. Art transports them from the darkness and sluggishness of everyday life to a better world. And yes, art has transfigured and immortalized whole eras of new cultural and historical development.

And this is why artists, endowed by God to be the ones who give meaning to the most important events in human life, have always walked hand in hand with other great people. Whenever culture and history have blossomed, the rule has always been that "the musician walks with the king."

This is not to say that all rising epochs of history had great artistic renaissances. On the contrary, usually these epochs follow one another. Either a flowering of arts and sciences precedes a great, historical change or great, historical changes precipitate a flowering of arts and sciences. It may be that, depending on the times, either historical change or arts and sciences draw all the outstanding and exciting personalities of the period to it, monopolizing and exhausting them. And maybe they do not recognize or are not able to express the other possibilities within themselves.

But one shouldn't generalize about this. There have been statesmen who were worlds apart from anything artistic, who were so one-sided and caught up in the technical side of life that they hardly had time, abilities, desire, or even enough energy for purely intuitive endeavors. They lacked deep empathy for the true nature of art; and this empathy is necessary to be able to serve art with warmth and passion or to fall under the spell that art casts.

There have been many great soldiers who were just soldiers and had no wish to be more.

Take, for instance, the extraordinary organizers, instructors, educators, and army officers, who have been influential enough to shake the world. These statesmen and soldiers changed history in ways that had nothing to do with anything related to art and thus affected the arts only indirectly.

It is different, however, with other statesmen and soldiers, whose personality and works are grounded more in feelings than in the intellect, who draw their strength from imagination rather than from rational thought. These people are truly great when it comes to shaping history; they stand close to the artistic side of things because they are made of the same elements. Future generations will see these people wonderfully and inexplicably manifested as personalities who followed their callings and used their gifts. They will be remembered for providing meaning and structure to destiny, although the true impact of this will not be obvious for many centuries.

In our own history, men like Friedrich the Great or the great Generalfeldmarschall von Moltke belong in this category of great historical figures. From the very beginning they were sensitive artistic souls by nature, who, as God's journeymen, stood at the loom as the times were being woven. They left their marks on history because they followed the inevitable dictates of their inner daemons. There is nothing wrong with the type of activity within the state and military that is more of a craft, as long as it is carried out conscientiously, industriously, energetically and doggedly. What would Friedrich the Great have been without Friedrich Wilhelm I, the father of soldiers and civil servants? Friedrich Wilhelm I had to be there so that the other could influence history as he wanted. One had to build the state that the other had started. One had to establish and drill an army for the other to move and lead through difficult, daring campaigns to victories that made history.

On the occasion of handing over a valuable manuscript that he had purchased, the treasures of the Bavarian State Library are shown to the Führer.

Keep in mind in this context, that if both are not united in one, the first, more creative one, is more highly valued historically than the purely organizational. Creation itself, when you come right down to it, is a product of artistic drive and usually stems from the deepest and most mysterious intuition. Friedrich, who wrote poetry and studied the most profound philosophical ideas, also stood in his tattered, filthy uniform at the bivouac fires of Leuthen in the midst of his grenadiers. And he knew how to elegantly hold a flute as well as how to wield a sword firmly and bravely in his hand.

There has never been a dearth of soldiers like these in the Prussian-German army. The unjust caricature of Prussian militarism depicted in the world has nothing to do with

Visiting an artist's studio in Munich. At Professor Wackerle's studio. Professor Troost's wife is in the middle.

65

Visiting the Schiller Haus in Weimar 1934.

the truth. Often, the solders trained at the War Academy or in the General Staff were not only military men but also philosophers.

Nowhere was the style of speech and writing more clear or more artistic than in the army training institutions.

German politics, however, always lacked these exciting and fascinating personalities. There were often good craftsmen who understood their craft, but there was nothing to them other than their craft. In our history Friedrich the Great, in his role as a soldier, had many counterparts who thought the way he did or moved in the same direction. In his role as a statesman, he is completely alone.

And this is what sets him apart as great and unique. This makes him someone with more than a mere aesthetic enjoyment of art. For him art was not an escape from life, but a way to face life when it became too hard and unbearable, or when he needed to draw energy and strength from somewhere else in order to get on with it. Art is not weak, and therefore it does not teach weakness. The strong principles of art provide strength and preserve this strength. Men who deep in their souls find art fulfilling are able to offer the nations of the world great lessons in politics and military strategy. They are also true artists. For them, politics and military leadership are nothing more than art-one art form among many to which these men are attached and to which they feel a deep connection.

The Führer as Statesman is one of those rare personalities so seldom seen in Prussian-German history. His deepest nature is rooted in the artistic. He is a builder by nature. He smiles when he says that even as a child he intended to build things. Little did he know that he would be called to build a state rather than houses. The most basic characteristics of his newly-built Reich follow the immortal principles of authentic architecture. His organization of the state shows natural logic at work. Everything comes together slowly and calmly following a far-sighted, carefully conceived plan. He works like a good builder who knows that Rome was not built in a day; that he has been called to create and to work for decades and centuries to come, not for the immediate future. This distinguishes the Führer's newly-built Reich from all previous attempts-it is based on permanence, and it is imbued with a principle of clarity that is almost architectural. In the new Reich, usefulness and beauty are united in rare harmony.

Long before he came to power, the Führer once said in a speech, "If German artists knew what I would one day do for them, all of them would stand by me!" These words went unheeded at the

The Führer in Bayreuth.

time. And without having to be reminded (as if by impatient creditors) of his words, the Führer fulfilled his promise much sooner than one would have dared to hope.

Hitler's inner need for art would have been obvious to others if they had observed him before the takeover, when he was in the midst of difficult political negotiations and tactical struggles. Together with a few comrades he would sit somewhere unnoticed in a theater box. Here, in the sublime notes of a Wagner opera, he heard the musical counterpart of his politics. There are few people today who have heard "Die Meistersinger" or "Tristan" as often as Hitler has. He is a fanatic about the arts. He does not subscribe, however, to the smugness of the middle-class, which hears something once and thinks it has understood and grasped the genius behind it. Hitler is filled instead with a deep and almost humble reverence when presented with the great gifts of man's artistic genius.

This reverence allows him to see and understand the man and his works as a whole. To see the Führer in the company of artists is to understand how deeply and personally he feels connected to them. To see the tireless care he takes of art and artists on a daily basis is to understand what art means to him. His reverence toward true artistic value is, as it were, a form of gratitude. Only those who are lucky enough to be allowed to help him know how important the Führer is for Richard Wagner's work in general and for Bayreuth in particular, as a patron, a friend, and advisor.

No one in the small group of people who are usually with him will ever forget, when he was still the leader of the opposition, the time he dashed off magnificent plans for the new architectural layout of Berlin and Munich with just a few cursory lines on a few loose pieces of paper. Everything was where it belonged, combining modern, technical thinking and the true strength of a builder. This was the first version of a new face for these cities, cleaned and purified of all the inappropriate, styleless, and tasteless features that the times had forced upon them.

The Führer leaves an artist studio at the Art Academy in Munich.

Members of the audience at the Bayreuth Festival greet the Führer.

The monumental party buildings, the new layout for Königsplatz, the German Art Museum in Munich, the ambitious, new layout of the Reich's capitol, all of which are already visible as projects in progress-these are the first manifestations of Hitler's early plan, which at the time had seemed almost farfetched. Outsiders would find it almost incomprehensible that the Führer not only provides the ideas and the initiative for these projects, which will take centuries to complete, but he also precisely

67

Drawings by Hitler while a soldier at the front: Ardoye in Flanders (summer 1917).

follows the implementation of his ideas down to the smallest detail. The Führer always has time for a blueprint. We often saw him in the studio of Professor Troost, the brilliant architect who unfortunately died so young. Here Hitler would sit enthusiastically looking at the blueprints and models that are now becoming reality built of stone. We are often permitted to accompany him to new buildings in different stages of completion. It is then that we see how joyful and moved he is when he inspects even the smallest things and the tiniest details because they fit into a universal order of meaning and purpose.

The pictures he painted in his youth are also filled with this spirit. They are complete down to the last line. They have the precision and meticulous exactitude of a trained architect. It is rumored that there are business-minded forgers who have truly mastered the skill of counterfeiting and copying these small works of art. But they cannot deceive a real expert. You can tell at a glance the difference between an original painting by the Führer and a copy, because the Führer speaks to us from the original. And you see in the original a germinal variation of all the artistic principles that appear later, monumental and magnificent, in the state he is building.

The same person who, as a young man in Vienna, went without many a meal to buy standing-room tickets to the Vienna Opera to hear Wagner or Mozart today beholds a painting or a sculpture with the same artistic passion. A lucky happenstance made it possible for him to purchase Böcklin's "Battle of the Centaurs." And later we watched him, reverent and humble in the presence of great art, sitting motionless for a long time in front of this work of genius.

Who could doubt that these noble passions are anything but the inevitable expression of the same artistic sensibility that shows itself in his work? Do his speeches not, for instance, document his vivid and intuitive Weltanschauung? Are they not like a classical building or a Bach fugue-beautifully structured with clarity of style? Are they not also monumental expressions of ideas, precise and multi-faceted? It is pathetic to try to understand someone by isolating one trait from his whole personality. And it is here that the individual traits come together to form a whole. And within this whole is the outline of an artistic and intuitive man. This is a man who is himself, who acts like himself, and could not be any different or act any differently even if he wanted to.

The Führer imbued his movement from the very beginning with the fiery impulse of modern thought that would later give him the strength to lead the movement to great victories. He did not make the movement a slave to technology. Instead, he consciously made technology serve the movement. The Führer is a proponent of technology. He uses it to support his goals and work. Technology, too, has its artistic side. A magnificently built bridge or a modern car built precisely according to virtually classical principles will always satisfy a desire for beauty. The highways, designed by the Führer and built by modern engineers according to the Führer's blueprints, are twentieth-century works of art. We can still picture the Führer on a sunny Sunday afternoon standing in front of the bold, monumental arch of the Mangfall Brücke. How his features mirrored his pride and satisfaction! This is a man who envisions immortal art coming from the most modern technical achievements of these important times.

The Führer is a sworn enemy of dilettantism; he is proud to be of the opinion that it is better to read, to see, or to hear one thing that is truly good and great ten times than it is to have ten times more variety of average or below average works. If he sees a great, artistic film, he will watch it again some other time. If a film is only average, he stops it within the first five or ten minutes.

No wonder all true artists deeply love and revere him. He is their friend and, when necessary, a generous protector. He cannot imagine life without art. Never was there a royal patron who was so open-minded about the arts. Where art is great and promising, he reaches out to it with his patronage. He never has a know-it-all attitude or tries to make up other people's minds for them. And he, who earned his way to art through hard material sacrifice as an impoverished construction worker, opens his heart and his wallet-especially when it is a matter of bringing art to the people and the people to art. Concepts like a "Theater of the People" have become reality under his patronage. He is a warm-hearted friend, an advisor, and guardian of the great German cultural organization "Strength through Joy." His sense of what is beautiful has none of that unpleasant, pseudo-aesthetic quality of hedonistic selfishness. His is a sense of what is simultaneously useful and what is universal.

Statesmen from other countries visited him recently in Berlin to discuss the reconstruction of Europe in long and difficult negotiations. Little did they know that the man who morning, noon, and afternoon defended German rights and who, as though he were an economist or military specialist, had every statistic and date at his fingertips, would be sitting that same evening with a small group of them in his apartment, and, moved to the depths of his soul, would be listening to the quintet from the third act of "Meistersinger" or a piece by Schubert, Schumann, or Wolf. Perhaps they thought that this man had suddenly become a dif-

Drawings by Hitler while a soldier at the front: a shelter in Fournes.

Watercolor by Hitler while a soldier at the front: ruins of a monastery in Messines (December 1914)

Watercolor by Hitler, soldier at the front: House with White Fence.

ferent person, that he had suddenly put on a face they had never seen before; and yet in reality he was the same-a statesman with unlimited spirit, a man with all the traits and all the potential of the German soul within him, an artist who sits among artists and feels kinship with them because he carries a piece of their innermost selves within him. Perhaps this short hour with him gave those who had the honor of participating a better idea of the Führer's innermost nature than the long hours spent in technical discussions and conferences. Here again was the fascinating strength of his true personality-that same personality which gave the great Prussian king strength in battle and to fight decisive wars, not in spite of the fact that he was a poet, but rather because he was a poet. It is the same personality as the great Prussian king who had embraced philosophy, built Sanssouci, played the flute and, when the rough business of the state and the military allowed him the time, gathered the most illustrious and best minds of Europe around his dinner table.

Here we see, coming together from apparent contradictions and differences, the final synthesis of a great human being and his works that will endure for centuries. Here art crosses over into military and state matters. The same power is at play here, it is simply influencing other areas. It uses the same kind of energy that drives and inspires art: imagination, instinct, grace, and inspiration. Perhaps the full extent of what this means for Germany, for our nation, and our national destiny will not be clear until sometime in the future. But it is we who have the great fortune of experiencing and feeling what it is like to have a true genius work and reign within us, over us, and around us. This great man's artistic feelings did not come from a desire for luxury or for play. His is a necessity in the true sense of the word, indispensable for life and work, for his very existence.

Perhaps the Führer is best and most deeply understood when observed in the midst of these situations. Art is for him a mysterious power that sparks the human heart to new love "in all the gray hours that life's wild circle weaves for us." And his connection with art and with artists, his care and his tireless guardianship for them, is nothing more than the payment and fulfillment of a debt and duty. This is what the poet means when he says, "Thou sublime art, I thank you for it!"

A watercolor by the Führer painted in 1914: The courtyard of the old residence in Munich.

The Führer leaves the building site of the German Art Museum.

The Buildings of the Führer
by Albert Speer, Architect

Frequently in history heads of state have shown strong support for the arts and especially for architecture. For example, to please the eye Rococo princes living in the eighteenth century commissioned castles and gardens and made it possible for the architects living at that time to create freely.

The Führer, as head of state, is building; but he will never be able to build in this traditional sense-for his great buildings, which are now emerging in many places, shall be an essential expression of the movement for centuries to come, and thus shall be a part of the movement in and of themselves. The Führer created this movement and came to power through its strength; and to this day he determines its ultimate structure, right down to the finest details. Therefore, unlike leaders of earlier centuries, he cannot build as a benevolent sponsor, and to an even lesser degree as a patron of the arts; he must build as a National Socialist. As a National Socialist he determines the cleanliness and purity of the building concept; the severity of the architectural expression; the clarity of the building design; and the quality of the material, just as he determines the intentions and the expression of the movement. Most importantly he determines the new inner spirit and therefore the true substance of his buildings.

Building is not a frivolous pastime for the Führer. It is a serious matter in which even stone material is intended to give distinct expression to the will of the National Socialist Movement.

It is unprecedented in the history of the German nation that a leader initiates at a critical turning point not only the greatest ideological and political reform of all time, but that he also-simultaneously and with the considered expertise of a master builder-works on creating stone monuments as well. These buildings shall document for centuries to come the political will and the cultural abilities of this great era.

Thus after many centuries of confusion, through this one resolution in building, a clarity and strength will be achieved which, with continued development, can result in a completely new stile of architecture.

In 1924 the Führer wrote in "Mein Kampf" that he had felt ever since his youth that social questions were closely connected to architecture.

"As soon as my interest in social issues was awakened, I began to study it in depth. It was a new, previously undiscovered world that opened up to me. For me it was only natural that by studying it, I was enthusiastically contributing to my love for architecture. Architecture, next to music, seemed to me the queen of arts. My activities related to architecture were under these circumstances in no way 'work', but instead the highest form of pleasure. I could read or draw late into the night without tiring. My belief strengthened that my beautiful dream for the future would become reality, if only after many years. I was convinced that I was going to make a name for myself as a master builder.

And he documents in the first chapter of "Mein Kampf" the importance of the deep impressions that his years in Vienna made on him.

"During this time I created for myself a perception

of the world and an ideology that became the granite foundation of my action at that time. I have had to learn little in addition to that which I had established for myself. I have not had to alter anything.

On the contrary.

I firmly believe today, that, in general, all creative thought develops principally during youth, if it is to develop at all."

The Führer never let go of this youthful love of architecture. But the foundation of the state and the life of the German nation were so disturbed because of war and revolution that Hitler, who even as a soldier was already becoming more and more involved in political issues, decided to become a politician.

He said, "Wouldn't it be ridiculous to build houses on that kind of a foundation?"

To him, becoming a politician was a sacred, serious and difficult decision, for it meant taking leave of architecture, the art form to which he personally remained faithful, and one with which he always remained involved. To this day it is his great love.

In the first turbulent years of his political struggle, at the same time during which he first gave structure to the movement, he gave final clear creative format to all symbolic modes of expression. He designed the swastika flag for the movement and for the German nation. He decided on the majestic eagle for the party, now the symbol of the German Reich's majesty. He developed the insignia of the SA and the SS. He developed a new structure for his many rallies, and thereby essentially determined the concept after which all buildings on the site of the Nuremberg NSDAP rally are modeled.

For the party rallies in Nuremberg he developed and determined in many meetings the ground rules and agenda. In addition, he spent hours thinking about careful guidelines for establishing each division of the party, about the treatment of the flags and about decorating the individual halls.

The Königsplatz in Munich after its renovations by Adolf Hitler.

The columned hall at the German Art Museum in Munich.

Design for the Congress Hall on the site of the Nuremberg Nazi Party rallies.

In Nuremberg, his faithful followers have saved and preserved his sketches and drawings from this period.

At a time when all his strength is focused on one important goal, involvement in art remains for him the "highest form of pleasure," and not "work."

Fate allowed him a timely encounter with master builder Paul Ludwig Troost. A friendship based on similarity of character soon developed. What Dietrich Eckart was to the Führer when it came to the exchange of ideological ideas, Professor Troost soon became in regard to architecture.

The first building to be created through the unique relationship between these two men, (although small, the first building of the movement) was the "Braunes Haus" on Brienner Street in Munich. Even though it was only a renovation, for the time it was an enormous project, as the Führer often said later. Here one can already see the characteristics that the buildings following the seize of power would express even more clearly: sharp and stern, but never monotonous. Simple and clear, and without fake ornamentation. Limited decorations, but every decorative element placed so properly that it would never be considered superfluous. All material, forms, and lines elegant.

The speaker podium in the Luipold arena at the site of the Nuremberg Nazi Party rally.

The plans for this renovation project came about in Troost's studio, located in a building on Theresien Street in Munich. Later, the plans for the Königsplatz in Munich and for the German Art Museum and many of the Führer's other buildings would be developed in this same studio, laying the foundation for a new attitude toward architecture. The Führer never worked on the plans for these important buildings in his administrative offices.

For years he has been driving to Troost's studio in his free time to lose himself completely in the plans of upcoming construction projects while physically removed from his political activities. The Führer involves himself not only in the general plans; every single detail and every new compilation of material comes under his scrutiny, and many things are improved because of his stimulating interest. The hours of planning together, as the Führer has often said, are hours of pure joy. They give him a sense of profound happiness, and provide him the most noble sort of relaxation during which he always finds new energy for other plans. Here he has the opportunity to dedicate himself to architecture during the few hours of free time left to him.

Many years before the takeover, Hitler and Troost discussed plans for the buildings that are just now being built. In the winter of 1931 to 1932 they were already discussing the future layout of the Königsplatz in Munich. Many fine sample drawings resulted from this collaboration. Even before the takeover of power the final plans for the Platz had been decided, and much of it was laid out in plans and models.

When, in 1932, the Glass Palace in Munich burned down and the then government proposed and decided on a bland design to replace it, the Führer, in addition to all of his other worries, had yet another one: that this imperfect plan would start before he was in power.

Comparing the model of the earlier design to the model of the German Art Museum, designed by Paul Ludwig Troost, one can see more clearly than

The Führer and Rudolf Heß view the building of the Führerhaus in Munich.

The buildings of the Führer are constructed in natural stone according to technically tested standards. Natural stone and northern brick are our sturdy building materials. Usually, the more expensive products are in the long run the most cost effective. Unlimited longevity is, according to all technical considerations, always the primary and most decisive quality. That is because the Führer's buildings are meant to represent our great era far into the future. Once the movement's and our state's immortal buildings are present in Germany's towns, they will be buildings that the people can be proud of. Everyone will know that the buildings belong to everyone. It will not be the department stores and the administrative buildings of banks and companies that will give cities their character, but rather the Führer's buildings, created by him.

The Führer writes the following about cities past and future:

"In the nineteenth century, our cities began more and more to lose the character of cultural centers, anywhere else how the Führer's ideas take form. Paul Ludwig Troost was the Führer's irreplaceable master builder until Trost's death. Troost knew how to capture Hitler's intentions and give them the correct architectural expression.

In his great speech at the National Socialist Party Assembly on Culture in 1935, the Führer erected a monument in honor of Professor Troost in a manner that could not have been more splendid for an architect of our time. He said:

"It should fill us with joyful pride that an act of destiny allowed the greatest master architect since Schinkel to build for the new Reich and for the movement his first, and unfortunately, only works in stone as monuments to a most noble, truly Germanic tectonic architecture."

It delights the Führer to see building plans develop. It is however an equal joy for him to witness the construction of these buildings.

Whenever he walks around one of his building sites, often accompanied only by a few colleagues, he becomes the field specialist. He asks many clearly phrased, technical questions, some about the foundation, about the strength of the walls, about difficult construction details that usually touch on some already existing unsolved difficulty. He often has suggestions, especially in technical areas; when the experts struggle to find a solution after discussing at length all the possibilities, Hitler's suggestion, generally totally different, always proves to be a clear and easy answer to the problem.

Every new development in architecture and every new detail receives his thorough assessment and approval. Despite his pleasure in details, he never forgets to pay attention to the generous alignment and lines which distinguish all of his buildings.

The "Ewige Wache" at the Königsplatz in Munich.

The foyer of the Opera House in Charlottenburg, in whose renovation the Führer participated.

The Führer, Professor Gall, and Architect Speer inspect the construction progress of the German Art Museum in Munich.

and began to sink to the level of mere human settlements.

When Munich's population reached 60,000, the city wanted to become one of Germany's first centers of culture. Today nearly every factory town claims this, as do cities with larger populations, but without having even the smallest thing of value to set it apart; nothing more than just a collection of apartments and rented barracks. How is anyone supposed to love a place that offers so little meaning. No one will feel especially tied to a city that has nothing more to offer than every other city, with no trace of individuality, where everything resembling art or culture has been meticulously avoided.

Not only that, but even the truly important large cities are becoming poorer in terms of important works of art as the populations constantly increase.

Modern times have contributed nothing to our major cities in terms of culture. All of our cities live on the glory and the treasures of the past.

Our major cities today do not have any monuments which dominate the city image, that somehow could be called a symbol of the whole era. Not so with the cities of antiquity, where almost every city had a monument to be proud of. The character of ancient cities lay not in private buildings but in public monuments. It seems these monuments were intended not for the moment, but for eternity, since they were supposed to reflect the greatness and meaning of the community, and not the wealth of a single owner.

Even in the Germanic Middle Ages the same principle was maintained, although the concept of art was completely different. What antiquity expressed in the Acropolis and the Pantheon was then cloaked in the form of the gothic cathedral.

But how truly pathetic the relationship between the state and private buildings has become today. If the same fate that struck Rome were to befall Berlin, subsequent generations would see the department houses of Jews and the hotels of a few businessmen as the great works of our time and as the characteristic expression of culture today.

Our cities at present lack an overarching symbol of national unity, so one can not wonder if those living in these cities lack a symbol within themselves."

It is in this sense that one must understand the Führer's great buildings at the Königsplatz, the German Art Museum in Munich, and the National Socialist assembly buildings in Nuremberg. They are the beginning, but none the less fundamental, and with the residential buildings of the Führer we are now also at the beginning of a new evolution. It is indeed logical that one thinks first of these major buildings whenever the Führer's projects are spoken of, considering the importance the Führer places on architecture.

But one should not assume that these projects exhaust the Führer's architectural activities.

On the contrary.

We know from his speeches how important it is to Hitler to improve the social conditions of all Germans in such a way that each individual can be proud of the achievements of the community as a whole. The Führer emphasizes the importance of housing in "Mein Kampf."

In his years living in Vienna, he learned first hand about the insufferable living conditions of working families.

He writes:

"In those days, I came to understand quickly and thoroughly what I had not suspected before. The nationalization of a people is first of all a question of creating healthy social conditions which act as a foundation for an environment in which it is possible for the individual to be educated.

Official statistics record the number of completed apartments either through new building projects or through renovations in the Reich.

1932	159,121
1933	202,113
1934	319,439

These numbers express better than words how sound housing has increased under the Führer's government. This increase will continue even more once "building plans necessary for our security have been completed. These projects cannot be postponed."

Then the monumental buildings of National Socialism will rise above the workers' sound dwellings and above the clean factories of our great cities, just as the cathedrals of the Middle Ages rose over the gabled roofs of private citizens' houses.

The tasks posed here are great, but the Führer filled us all with courage when he said in his speech at the National Socialist Assembly on Culture:

"The people will rise to these lofty responsibilities. We do not have the right to doubt that if the Almighty gives us the courage to pursue immortality, he will also give our people the strength to create that which is immortal."

Engagement on the new alpine road.

Adolf Hitler and His Roads
by Inspector General Fritz Todt, Doctor of Engineering

Those who have come to know the Führer in the preceding articles as statesman, orator, the leader of the movement and of other activities may wonder: In these very troubled times, does this statesman, this politician, does the head of state of the German Reich really have the interest and time to concern himself personally with an abstract technical matter such as road construction? The following notes should give the reader an idea of the extent of the Führer's commitment to his roads.

The Concept

Even while in Landsberg Prison the Führer spoke about the necessity of building roads to meet the needs of the automobile. In this context he also planned someday to connect Germany's Gaue by roads.

During his fourteen-year political struggle, the Führer almost exclusively used the automobile in his travels, getting to know the German highways running north to south and east to west. It never ceases to amaze us how well the Führer knows entire routes, their character, their development, suitable rest stops, and other details. The Führer particularly values automobile trips overland because no other means of transportation allows the traveler as close a connection to the nation and countryside as the automobile. Someone once tried to add up how many kilometers the Führer had covered on German highways during the fourteen years of his political struggle. It was certainly 500,000 to 700,000 kilometers, probably more. In other words, the distance the Führer has covered in an automobile on German highways is twelve to fifteen times greater than the circumference of the earth. These trips resulted in a thorough concept for the construction of a connected system of roads strictly for automobiles. This concept was fully developed by the time he seized power.

Twelve days after being appointed Reich's Chancellor-in his first public speech at the opening of the Automobile Show on February 11, 1933-the Führer announced the beginning of an ambitious road construction plan and other measures to promote motorization. He said:

"Just as the horse-drawn vehicle once had its own routes and the railroad built railroad lines as necessary, motor traffic must also have the highways it requires. In earlier times a nation's standard of living was often measured by the number of kilometers of railroad line. In the future then the number of kilometers of roads for the automobile driver will be the standard."

Just under three months passed between that February 11 and the first National Labor Day in the new National Socialist Reich on May 1 – a time that was filled with the consolidation of the power gained on January 30. On this spring day in the countryside, the sun rose higher for the German nation once more. The Führer spoke of turning away from previous disunity, of eliminating unemployment, of the honor of work, and of beginning to work together, all of which – when oriented toward one will – is the prerequisite and basis for strengthening a nation. Toward the end of this first speech on the early organization of the Reich, the Führer said, "We are beginning a program that we do not want to leave for future generations to finish. This program is the construction of our roads, a gigantic task that will require billions. We will clear away the obstacles and begin on a grand scale." And so May 1 also marked the dawning of the road construction program. The Führer's concept was the transformation of will into action.

In subsequent weeks, the Führer met with German and foreign experts to gather information. He demanded that the cabinet do what it could to help realize his plans. The obstacles he had referred to in his May 1 speech were tackled in numerous meetings. On June 28, the cabinet passed a law establishing the Reich's autobahn project.

A few days later, the Inspector General for German Autobahn Engineering was appointed at a short, three-minute reception held by the Reich's Chancellor.

The Inspector General's Introduction

July 5 was probably the hottest day in the summer of 1933 in Berlin. The summer heat lasted weeks, and the stone buildings of the capital absorbed so much heat during the day that the short nights had no cooling effect. As happened every day, the receptions in the chancellery began at 10 o'clock in the morning. Day after day, these receptions would drag on late into the evening with only a short break at midday. Hour after hour, ministers, gauleiters (party district leaders), work-

At the Mangfallbrücke in the summer of 1935.

er delegations, industrialists, Germans living abroad, and many others came in shifts to make presentations to the Führer. There were probably some in the anteroom who promised that their presentations would not last longer than ten minutes. But the Führer takes up the topic himself, states his position on it, explains the issues completely, and participates just as actively in the last presentation late in the evening as he did in the first one.

The newly appointed Inspector General was first summoned by the Führer for an introduction at one o'clock in the afternoon. However, as so often happens, the schedule had been shifted in the course of the morning because of meetings running late. The appointment was postponed until seven o'clock in the evening on the grounds that "the Chancellor wishes to speak to you last, so that he will have time for this."

The Inspector General reported shortly before nine o'clock, right after the next-to-last visitor. The Chancellor said "Come with me to the garden. I must now finally get some fresh air." During a one-and-a-half hour walk in the garden of the chancellery, the Führer introduced his ideas to his Inspector General, spoke of impending developments in transportation, of the shortcomings of any measures designed to merely meet the current transportation requirements, and of long-term construction and work. He warned of obstacles and difficulties, gave technical details, determined precisely the minimum width a road could be; he insisted on the highest quality, and in general mapped out the lines for the main system. He finally dismissed the Inspector General repeating, "I believe this is necessary. I believe it is right to begin this project. You must believe in it just as firmly as I do and act accordingly without wavering."

Landmark at the beginning of the Munich - National Border Autobahn.

Breaking Ground, Frankfurt am Main, September 23, 1933

Planning and drafting took two and a half months of extremely intensive work. Frankfurt am Main was the only place ever considered as the starting place of the great work that stretched across all of Germany. Some years earlier, a research group there had theoretically looked into plans for a road meant to be strictly for automobiles from Hamburg through Frankfurt to Basel. This preliminary work made it possible to complete the draft work at an accelerated pace.

The plans for the first sections from Frankfurt to Darmstadt were complete in early September. The groundbreaking and the beginning of construction for this great work were set for September 23. In the very first meetings with the Inspector General, the Führer had already determined that he himself would start the construction. For years, the number of unemployed in Frankfurt had been increasing so that in 1932 it was up to around 80,000. And now the Führer's

Opening the first section of the Munich – National Border Reich's Autobahn.

The Führer's commitment to building roads. Inspecting Alpenstraße.

the embankment from which the Führer spoke. The guests of honor got somewhat less than their fair share of seats. But the workers were also the guests of honor here. The Führer said:

"Today, we stand at the beginning of a massive task. Its significance – not only for German transportation, but for the German economy in the broadest sense – will only be fully appreciated in later decades... In future decades people will see that transportation is dependent on the new, great autobahns that we will build throughout all of Germany... I know that this day of celebration will pass, that the times will come when rain, frost, and snow will make the work miserable and difficult. But it is necessary. The work must go on. No one will help us if we do not help ourselves."

The Führer closed his speech as follows:

"Go now to your job! Construction must begin today. The work commences! And before too much time goes by, an enormous achievement shall bear witness to our will, our industriousness, our ability, and our initiative. German workers, begin the work!"

After his speech to the jubilant workers the Führer seized his spade and stepped up to the construction site. A convoy of trucks rolled up with large, completely filled two-cubic-meter wagons. The wagons dumped the dirt with a loud thud at the foot of an embankment that would one day be six meters high. The Führer drove his spade robustly into the hard clods of earth, striking the pile over and over. This was no symbolic groundbreaking, this was real groundwork!

Several workers realized that the Führer would probably keep working until the two-cubic-meter pile was thoroughly leveled out. They rushed over with their shovels to help. And the Führer shov-

great construction project was to begin in the immediate vicinity of this city, creating steady work for thousands of workers. This brought confidence and faith back into the lives of the workers and their families. Bright and early, at seven o'clock in the morning, the first 700 workers marched off from the employment office. At the Börsenplatz, gauleiters and the Inspector General passed out tools. From there the workers went out to the Main, to the new work site, with music and jubilation.

The Führer arrived at ten o'clock by airplane. He had the greatest difficulties on his trip through Frankfurt. The SA, instead of providing a barricade, was cheering the Führer on, so the people of Frankfurt, young and old, got around the barricade again and again. The trip from the airfield to the work site took more than an hour.

The location of the groundbreaking was not a fairground, but a construction site. The workers and their families stood at the edge of

Engagement on the new alpine road.

eled with them until the pile of earth was properly leveled, and the first drops of sweat had fallen from his brow to the ground. Laughing, the Führer and two unnamed workers stopped when there was nothing left to shovel. He went through the work sites where in the meantime the remaining 700 workers had started working. "Did you see how the Führer even shoveled away the dirt from the track so that the wagons could be pulled out? Like a real excavator. He sure can work. I could hardly keep up," recounted one of the two afterwards.

A week after that groundbreaking a foreman came to the chief engineer in charge of the Reich's autobahn project and said, "Sir, we must put a fence up around the place where the Führer broke ground. At quitting time, our workers are taking pocketfuls of dirt home with them. Women and children are taking it away too." And so the Führer's work and the ethos of the workers had raised the status of a job that had previously been considered one of the filthiest. Today many workers' families from Frankfurt carefully preserve a small packet of soil as a prized possession.

The Führer's participation

The Inspector General reports to the Führer regularly on the progress of the work. The Führer makes decisions about details, in order to influence the basic attitude of the workers on this project. Again and again in these meetings over details it eventually becomes clear that the Führer's decisions are the only possible solution.

One example of this is a decision about where to lay the road along a section on the south shore of the Chiemsee in Upper Bavaria. There was marsh several kilometers wide between the lake and the rising mountains. It had been very difficult to cross this marsh when the railroad was being built. The first draft for the Reich's autobahn avoided the marsh by curving away from the lake's shore to the

Adolf Hitler's roads lead him to the people.

south. The Führer did not like this route. It had no view of the lake or the mountains, and he felt that it was not very well situated in the countryside. He demanded a more exhaustive examination into the possibility of locating the road closer to the lake. At his instigation extensive drilling was begun near the lake. We were greatly surprised to find a rock-like layer of molasse very close to the shore, just wide enough to run the road close to the lake's shore as the Führer wanted.

It was usually also the Führer who made the final decisions in selecting the design of large bridge-head structures. One of first really large projects that was tackled was Mangfall Brücke near Munich, approximately 300 meters long and 60 meters above the valley floor.

The Führer chose from among 70 drafts submitted in a competition and decided which one would be used. This was to become a model for the construction of large bridges used later in several other places. The lines and shape of the structures that the Führer chose are clear and simple, generous and bold. In addition to determining the shape, he also had significant influence regarding the issue of soundness of construction. The Führer rejected cheap structural components, such as hollow supports and piers, because he was concerned about durability. Like everything else, he did not build for the moment, but rather for the future. "What we build must still be standing long after we are no longer around." Sometimes the Führer disapproves of something too. He expresses his disapproval perfectly clearly. In one case, the Führer was so clear about stopping work on an unsuccessful building that he placed a phone call to the Inspector General who terminated operations immediately. It was the Führer himself also who made the decisions regarding the route and many other details for the Alpenstraße.

Opening the Reich's autobahn from Frankfurt to Darmstadt in 1935. From left to right: Reich's Minister of War von Blomberg, the Führer, Inspector General Dr. Todt, Reichsbank President Dr. Schacht, General Director of the State Railroad Dr. Dorpmüller, Reich's Minister of Propaganda Dr. Goebbels

Model camp for workers on the Reich's Autobahns

The start of construction work all over the Reich during 1934 made it necessary for some workers to be accommodated in barracks. At first these work camps were set up the way construction workers' accommodations had been for decades. In the summer, this style of camp was only barely sufficient. As winter drew near, urgent remedial measures appeared necessary, since these accommodations were inadequate for the workers on Adolf Hitler's roads. Repeated exhortations to industry were only partially successful. It was difficult to quickly and effectively convince people that these long-accepted accommodations had major shortcomings. Finally, the Inspector General came to the Führer for instructions about what to do. When the Führer learned that the barrack accommodations of the workers on his roads left something to be desired, he put his well-known energy to work, refusing to compromise, and within a few hours changes were being made. With the assistance of the Labor Service, model camps were set up within a few weeks all over Germany. Workers on Adolf Hitler's roads have clean accommodations in these model camps. Meals are taken in the larger rooms. Each camp has large washing and shower facilities with hot and cold water. There is an entertainment room for after work. The Führer himself sketched out the details of these camps. Because of the Führer's intervention in the fall of 1934, the German workers' accommodations reached a level that no other European country can even approach.

Seeing the Führer for the first time.

The Führer at construction sites and on the new roads

The Führer derives great joy from inspecting construction sites. He is interested in everything on the site: the operation, the building, and the worker accommodations. He is particularly interested in the location of the road in the countryside. The Führer wants his roads to be bold and wide, but at the same time in harmony with the countryside. The workers are usually very surprised when he suddenly appears among them. Some are so surprised that they actually drop their picks. And then their eyes beam with sheer joy that the Führer has come to their workplace. It is impossible to imagine the happiness and joy that prevails over a construction site when Hitler visits. The faces of hundreds of grown men remind us of the joy expressed by children when they see a Christmas tree. As a rule the workers stay where they are and continue to work after their initial surprise. This is their opportunity to show what they do. The Führer speaks with individuals, especially with older workers. It is not unusual to find septuagenarians at the construction site. The Führer told one 70-year-old worker near Darmstadt "When I am as old as you are, I hope I am still able to work like you now."

The Führer is delighted when he drives along completed sections of the road for the first time. He is incredibly interested in traffic counts, since they confirm that private individuals and businesses are interested in the new roads. The Führer inaugurated the section of autobahn from Heidelberg to Frankfurt am Main with a picnic. A few days before opening the road to traffic, he made the first trip on it on his way from Central Baden to the Rhineland. After the Inspector General's announcement, the Führer decided that they would take a break at a suitable picnic spot. In the magnificent, autumnal beech forest, the Führer's convoy left the road and Proviantminister Kannenberg conjured up his "magic table" in the forest. Third parties relate how enthusiastically the Führer recounts his trips on these newly completed roads.

Adolf Hitler has a close bond with the roads he is creating. He himself has constantly emphasized the important part the completed roads will play in the future development of transportation. And more: In a few years these roads will be a powerful propaganda tool. Motor traffic, and the manufacturing that goes with it, will increase to an extent that cannot even be anticipated today. In addition, our autobahns will attract many hundreds of thousands of foreigners each year. After the completion of the Reich's autobahns, Germany will be blessed with by far the most modern system of highways in the world." (February 15, 1935- Opening of the Automobile Show)

Far beyond Germany's borders, foreign countries are following our Führer's road construction. Individuals and groups of foreign guests make appointments to visit the construction sites or completed sections of the Reich's autobahns almost weekly. The enthusiasm and admiration is expressed in their letters and newspapers by the way they follow the expansion of the Führer's gigantic project. One of many foreign press offices writes "As the pyramids tell the story of the pharaohs, and the Roman roads bear witness to the power of the Roman emperor, so will these wonderful autobahns forever remind the German nation of the most extraordinary figure in its history, of a comrade, once without name and position, who – out of nothing and with no outside help, but on his own strength – created a new Reich and stamped his will on the destiny of an entire nation."

The Führer sails on the Rhine during the 1934 Saarland rally at Ehrenbreitstein.

In the city of the National Socialist Party Assemblies. In the window of Deutscher Hof Hotel in Nuremberg.

Our Hitler
Radio speech to the German nation on the Führer's birthday
By Dr. Joseph Goebbels

Although the Führer is often obligated, as a representative of the party and the people, to appear at mass rallies, receptions, or official celebrations and to speak to thousands or hundreds of thousands, he nevertheless consciously avoids all demonstrations and tributes that apply only to him and his person. As a result, he has always spent his birthday in some small village or little town in Germany. No one knows his whereabouts in advance. The Führer's purely human and personal manner strongly affects his closest staff members, as this radio address demonstrates. It was given by Reich's Minister Dr. Goebbels on the Führer's birthday, and was heard by the German nation over all German transmitters. The text of the third address, from April 20, 1935, deserves to be recorded in print particularly given the scope of this book.

National comrades! Two years ago, on April 20, 1933, when Adolf Hitler had been in power just under three months, I gave a radio speech to the German nation on the Führer's birthday. Now as then, it is not my intention to read out a flaming editorial. That I shall leave to better stylists than I. Nor do I endeavor to appraise the official work of Adolf Hitler. On the contrary: today, on the Führer's birthday, I feel that it is time to place Hitler, the man, before the eyes of the entire nation, so that the entire nation will know the magic of his personality, the enigmatic genius and irresistible force of his influence. Indeed, on this earth there is no longer anyone who does not know him as a statesman and a superior popular leader. However, only a few have a chance to see and experience him as a person at close proximity on a daily basis and, I would like to add, to learn to understand and love him all the more as a result. These few people understand: Why and how it is possible that a man, who just three short years ago was opposed by half the nation, has risen today above every doubt and every criticism in the eyes of the entire population. If Germany had never before found heart-stirring unity in one man, we have found it now in the conviction that Adolf Hitler is a man of destiny, who carries within him a calling to lead the nation from its terrible internal disintegration and disgraceful foreign political humiliation to longed-for freedom.

The fact that a man faced with this task has won the heart of the whole nation (which at times has required very difficult and unpopular decisions) is perhaps the deepest and most wonderful secret of our time. It cannot be explained just by purely objective accomplishments, for those who sacrificed the most for him and for his national reconstruction, and who still must sacrifice, are the very ones who have welcomed his mission most profoundly and joyfully. And they stand by him, as a leader and as a man, with sincere and fervent love. This is a result of his magic personality and the deep mystery of his pure and unadulterated

A final visit shortly before Hindenburg's death in July, 1934.

humanity.

It is this humanity, which reveals itself most genuinely to those who are most closely associated with him, that I will address here.

His humanity, like all genuine humanity, is clear and simple in essence as well as in action. This principle is as true for the smallest circumstances as it is for the largest. The simple clarity which shapes his political image is also the dominant principle of his entire life. It is hard to imagine him with any pretenses at all. If he were pretentious his people would not recognize him. His daily meals are the simplest and most unpretentious imaginable. His meals are always served the same way, regardless of whether he is eating with a few close friends or with important official visitors. Recently, during a reception for the Gauleiter of the Winter Welfare Organization, an old party member asked him after the midday meal to sign a menu as a souvenir. He hesitated a moment and then said, laughing, "Why not? The menus here never change, and it doesn't matter who sees them."

Adolf Hitler is one of the few heads of state who never wears medals or badges of honor except for a single war decoration, awarded for exceptional personal bravery when he was a simple soldier. This is a sign of modesty, but also of pride. No man under the sun could honor Hitler except Hitler himself. Every form of ostentation is abhorrent to him; but when representing the country and his nation, he does so with impressive, unflappable dignity. And behind everything that he is and does stand the words that the great soldier Schlieffen wrote about his work "More than it appears to be!" This has to do with superhuman diligence and tenacity to pursue set goals. When I arrived in Berlin a few days ago at one in the morning after two exhausting days of work, I wanted to sleep, but I was called to him to give a report. At two o'clock in the morning he sat there in his home, still fresh, surrounded by work, listening to a report almost two hours long about the building of the Reich's autobahn.

This topic seemed completely removed from the great foreign policy problems that had occupied him for the entire day, from early morning until late into the night. Before the last National Socialist Party Assembly in Nuremberg, I was his guest for a week in Obersalzberg. There was light shining from his window every night until six or seven in the morning. The Führer was dictating the great speeches he would give several days later at the party congress. He thoroughly studies the smallest detail of every potential law before the government adopts it. He is a military expert with extensive training; he has a specialist's knowledge of every weapon and every machine gun. If you are reporting to him about something, you must be ready with the smallest details.

Memorial service for Generalfeldmarschall von Hindenburg in the Courtyard of Honor at the Tannenberg Memorial. The Führer's eulogy.

His method of working is geared completely toward clarity. Nothing is more foreign to him than nervous hustle and hysterical exaggeration. He knows better than anyone else that there are a hundred or more problems to be solved. And so he selects two or three in particular which he sees as universal problems. While dealing with these, he doesn't allow himself to be distracted by the severity of the remaining problems. He knows full well that once the few major problems are resolved, the second and third-order problems almost solve themselves.

By attacking the problems himself, however, he illustrates, on the one hand, how tough one must be to battle through the fundamental issues, and how flexible the evaluating methods must be. The Führer is a stickler for principles, and he is a disciple of dogma; but he tackles these issues with superior pliability of means and methods. This is why principles and dogma never get short shrift with him. His goals have never changed. He is accomplishing today what he wanted in 1919. But the methods he has developed to carry out his goals have always varied depending on the situation. When he was offered the Vice Chancellorship in August of 1932, he declined point-blank with brief, simple words. He felt that the time was not yet right, and that the ground he would have stood on would not be enough to support him. When a wider door to power opened to him on January 30, 1933, he walked courageously through it, even though he wasn't given complete responsibility. He knew that the foundation on which he then stood was sufficient to begin a battle for complete power. The know-it-alls out there did not understand either of his decisions; today they owe him humble apologies. He was superior to them in terms of tactics as well as in the strategic use of principles. But in a display of short-sightedness, those with less insight arrogantly criticized those who advocated these principles.

In the past summer two photographs found their way into the press, showing the Führer in complete solitude at his most heart-wrenching. The first picture showed him on the day after June 30, when he had bloodily dealt with betrayal and mutiny, greeting the Reichswehr as they marched past the window of the chancellery. His face is almost numb from the sharp bitterness of the difficult hours he had just experienced.

The second photograph shows him leaving the house of the Reich's president in Neubeck after his final visit to the dying general field marshal. His face is overshadowed with pain and sorrow over the merciless death that in a few hours will tear his fatherly friend from him. On New Year's night, in an almost prophetic vision, he had already pre-

The morning of January 15, 1935. The Führer thanks Gauleiter Bürckel on the occasion of the victory in the Saar.

dicted to close circles the dangers he anticipated in the year 1934. He even predicted that Hindenburg would be taken from us that year. Now the inevitable was upon us. And the pain of an entire nation was expressed, not plaintively but in mourning, in the stone-like face of one individual.

The entire nation clings to him with reverence and with deep heartfelt love. The people feel that he belongs to them – flesh of their flesh and spirit of their spirit. This is expressed in the smallest and most trivial everyday things. For example, a respectful camaraderie prevails in the chancellery, inextricably connecting everyone – down to the last SS men in the escort party – to the Führer. When they travel, they all sleep at the same hotel and under the same conditions. Is it any wonder that the most unassuming people around him are precisely those who have turned out to be the most loyal? They feel instinctively that everything is the result of his natural inner spirit and unaffected mental attitude; nothing is posturing or pretense.

Several weeks ago approximately fifty young German women living abroad, who had just spent a year attending courses in the German Reich and now had to return to their troubled homelands, asked for permission to see him at his chancellery. He invited all of them to eat supper with him, and they spent hours telling him about their homes and their modest little lives. While saying their good-byes, they suddenly struck up the song "Wenn alle untreu werden" and they wept. In their midst stood the man who had become for them the personification of an eternal Germany, providing them with friendly, kindly words of consolation to take along with them on their difficult path.

He came from the people, and he is still one of the people. This man, who deliberated for two days in fifteen-hour meetings with statesmen from the world-power England, using masterful dialectic and hard statistics to settle Europe's destiny, is as natural and comfortable when speaking to the man on the street, immediately putting everyone at ease. This same man uses the intimate "du" when he addresses old soldiers, soldiers who have been worrying for days how they would address him and what they would say to him. The least important person approaches Hitler confidently knowing that he is a friend and protector. The people love him because they feel as safe and secure in his care as a child in the arms of its mother.

The Führer on his 47th birthday.

This man is fanatic about his work. He has sacrificed his happiness and private life for his work. For him, nothing is more fulfilling. He serves with a deep inner humility as the most loyal worker for the Reich. An artist becomes a statesman, and his great artistic genius manifests itself in his contribution to history. He does not need to have people honor him; his work itself honors him in a most lasting and immortal way. Those of us who have the privilege of seeing him on a daily basis receive nothing but light from his light. We want only to be his obedient followers in the procession led by his flag. He has frequently said to a small circle of his oldest comrades and closest confidants, "It will be terrible when some day the first of us dies and there is an empty place that no one else can fill." If fate is kind, his place will be occupied the longest, so that the nation can continue along this path to new freedom, greatness, and power under his leadership for many decades to come. In gratitude today the entire German nation lays this sincere and most ardent wish at his feet. Those of us who stand gathered closely around him and the last man in the most remote village now proclaim at this hour:

"He is now who he always was,
and who he is, he shall remain:
Our Hitler!"

Bückeberg, 1934.

The army of workers, National Socialist Party Assembly, 1935.

Reich's President von Hindenburg and Reich's Chancellor Hitler.

Memorial Day, 1935 at the war memorial in Berlin.

National Socialist Party Assembly, 1935: Soldier workers.

Germany today.

The Führer and the Wehrmacht
by First Lieutenant Foertsch

Adolf Hitler was a soldier in the German army. He served willingly with all his heart in the greatest war ever fought by any army. For four years he fought in the raging slaughter of world war, in filth and slime amidst the rain of bullets and clouds of gas. He fought on the front line – the front line that bled to death for the homeland.

He was a remarkable observer. He understood what the November Revolt could not have (but should have) grasped to prevent this activity from being immediately revealed as an outrageous betrayal of the nation. That is to say, he understood that a nation that cannot protect the workplace of its lowliest citizen from enemy attack cannot function. It can't work the soil if the sword doesn't protect the plough. He also saw where the old army was lacking. He saw how the Reichstag had sinned against it in the liberal days of 1914.

Two basic necessities became clear to him. One was to recreate German military freedom while simultaneously building a new German Wehrmacht strong enough to protect Germany's borders against attack. The second was to build up this Wehrmacht based on the old approaches to general military service. This philosophy assumes that military service is an honor to the nation, and therefore anyone unworthy or foreign should not be awarded this honor. But neither should any individual be given preference or special rights.

The Führer took a personal interest in the German Wehrmacht and was satisfied to see that it was possible for the Reichswehr to keep it in shape in the midst of the pacifism and defeatism, betrayal and corruption of the November Republic. He even saw that it could be forged into a useful weapon.

And so, early on, the Reichswehr and the NSDAP's Führer formed a bond. The younger officers soon recognized that Hitler was the only man capable of re-establishing the German army.

A few days after January 30, 1930 the Führer, recently named Chancellor, assembled all the high commanders of the Wehrmacht at the Reichswehr ministry. He detailed the basic tenets of National Socialist policy for them. He gave them their assignments, showed them where they fit into the picture of what he wanted from the Wehrmacht, and showed them what the Wehrmacht's purpose in National Socialist Germany would be. Nothing that transpired in this meeting was made public. It was still not the time to draw attention to these questions. It would be another two years before the new German Wehrmacht could come out into the bright light of day.

In his book, "Mein Kampf," Hitler honors the old army where he had served for four years as a simple soldier and later as a corporal. The words he uses to honor this experience express his great pride in the German Wehrmacht now and forever: "The army was the most powerful school for the German nation. Our enemies hated this particular shield of national self-preservation and freedom for good reason. There can be no greater memorial to this single institution than to accept the fact that it was slandered, hated, fought, and feared by all those inferior beings. We can summarize in one word what the German nation can thank the army for: everything! The army taught absolute responsibility in an age where responsibility was very rare indeed. It taught personal courage in an age where cowardice threatened to become a raging sickness. The willingness to sacrifice, to initiate oneself for the general good was looked upon as stupidity. Only those who knew how to protect and further themselves were considered intelligent. The army was the school that still taught individual Germans that the wellbeing of the nation cannot be found in the lies of our international brothers, but in the power and unity of our own nation.

The army taught decisiveness at a time when indecisiveness and doubts dominated people's lives elsewhere. It was not easy to

Wehrmacht Day in Nuremberg, 1935: Anti-aircraft guns in formation.

Anti-aircraft battery telemetry on Wehrmacht Day at the National Socialist Party Assembly, 1935.

Protecting the coast: Navy artillery for coastal defense.

Launching ceremony of the Panzer ship "Admiral Graf Spee".

The Führer among his young men in blue.

Visiting the fleet.

maintain discipline at a time when so many set an example of an undisciplined life. There is an unspoiled, robust healthiness in this fundamental principle. It would have disappeared from our daily lives a long time ago if the army and the army's teaching had not provided continuous renewal of this basic force. The army taught idealism and devotion to the great Vaterland. It espoused a united nation instead of separation into classes. Probably the only thing wrong with the army was the one-year voluntary enlistment policy. However, much credit must be given to the army of the old Reich. It stood above the majority in an age of majority rule. Compared to the Jewish-Democratic blind worship of numbers, the army believed in the individual. The army educated men, and this was what these new times needed most. Despite the spreading swamp of emasculation and feminism, the army produced 350,000 powerful young men from its ranks each year. These young men shed their youthful weakness and developed strong bodies during their two-year education. Only those who learned to obey during this time also learned how to give orders. A German soldier could be recognized by the way he walked. This was the German nation's foremost school. The army was hated (and for good reason) by those who, out of jealousy or greed, wanted a powerless Reich with defenseless citizens. Many Germans, blinded by hate or delusions, did not want to see what the outside world already knew: the German army was the most powerful force available to help Germany obtain freedom and nourishment for its children.

However, there was a reason that the Führer felt this could not be

93

transferred from the old army into the new Wehrmacht in accordance with the Treaty of Versailles. This treaty was not designed to satisfy the will of the nation. It was forced upon the nation in its present form by outsiders. Only two citizens per thousand of the entire population were allowed to serve in the military. This meant of course that the Wehrmacht would not be allowed to have this all-encompassing effect of educating the nation.

For the Führer, it was obvious that this kind of regular army was not a real people's army. The soldiers knew this too. It is no surprise, then, that the Wehrmacht enthusiastically greeted the decision of von Hindenburg, the president of the Reich at that time, to make the Führer chancellor. If any power in Germany could free the army and navy from the shackles of Versailles, it was the power of this chancellor. The strongest political movement of the nation was marching behind him.

In the ranks of the Reichswehr, however, it was clear that this act of freedom would not be child's play. They must reckon with extreme difficulty. But they had rock solid trust that the Führer, and

*National Socialist Party Assembly in Nuremberg, 1935.
The flags of the glorious old army on Wehrmacht Day.*

no one but the Führer, was capable of pulling it off. When on October 14, 1933 Hitler announced the decision to leave the League of Nations, every soldier's heart went out to him in joy. They realized that was the beginning of re-establishing German military freedom.

It is no accident that the German army has marched beside the SA and party formations on every German holiday since that momentous day in Potsdam. This new army is a true people's army. The army no longer looks at differences in descent, ability, or social position, just as the party

Proclamation of military freedom, 1935.

Swearing in new recruits to the people's army at the Feldherrnhalle in Munich on November 7, 1935.

The Führer with the Reich's Minister of War and the Supreme Commander of the army in 1935 at maneuvers, Munsterlager troop exercise grounds.

Bomber over Nuremberg.

First visit to the Richthofen Squadron.

The arrival of German troops on the Mainz Bridge over the Rhein, March 7, 1936.

New tanks.

never has. The army now belongs to the people, and it belongs right in the middle. And so, although it is not a rule, it is taken for granted that the army will be at center stage on the nation's holidays. This is true of all holidays – the First of May, Harvest Day, a festive or sad occasion, or great Nuremberg Volkstag. No matter what the occasion, the Wehrmacht is there among the people.

In his great Reichstag speech on January 30, 1934, the anniversary of the National Socialist Revolution, the Führer said these words about the Wehrmacht's role in it:

"It is a unique historical event that, to serve the nation, such heartfelt unity has arisen between the forces of the revolution and the leaders of a most disciplined Wehrmacht. Much like the bond between the National Socialist Party and myself as its Führer on the one hand, and my bond with the soldiers of the German Reich's army and navy on the other, the Wehrmacht and its leaders stand beside the new state with total trust."

The Wehrmacht is not a separate entity. Rather, it is a National Socialist Wehrmacht. This goes

"Lützow" tower and the battle mast of the "Admiral Scheer" as seen from the port bow.

Our Air Force.

without saying in a National Socialist state. This is most proudly expressed when everyone serving in the Wehrmacht, from the Supreme Commander to the newest recruit, wears the National Socialist emblem on his shirt.

The Führer has emphasized this often and has identified the party and the Wehrmacht as the two pillars on which the National Socialist Third Reich is based. He has identified the party as the political arm of the nation, and the Wehrmacht as the military arm. Consciously, without being forced, and moved by a deep inner power, the Wehrmacht embraced the whole concept of the new National Socialist state and bonded with it. There is an uninterrupted continuity from the introduction of the NSDAP greeting, to participation in all party and state celebrations, to the introduction of the

Wehrmacht Day, 1935: The Führer with his commanders (left to right: Generaloberst Göring, Commander of the Air Force; Generalfeldmarschall von Blomberg, Commander of the Wehrmacht; Generalfeldmarschall Baron v. Fritsch, Commander of the Infantry; Generaladmiral Dr. h. C. Raeder, Commander of the Navy).

National Socialist Assembly in Nuremberg, 1935. The navy in procession on Wehrmacht Day.

Wehrmacht emblem, to participation in party assemblies, and to raising a battle flag adorned with the swastika. The "duties of the German soldier" are written with National Socialist spirit, as is the oath of allegiance; "I swear to God and all that is holy my absolute obedience to the leader of the German Reich and nation, Adolf Hitler, the Supreme Commander of the Wehrmacht. As a steadfast soldier I will be prepared to risk my life at all times on behalf of this oath."

From the first day in office, the Minister of War made it clear that the German Wehrmacht would be founded on the Weltanschauung of the National Socialists. Whenever he spoke to troops or to other groups he emphasized that this pledge of trust to the Führer was sincere and unwavering. The Wehrmacht was deeply engrossed in the rebirth of the German state. The Minister of War himself once said in an article in the *Voelkschen Beobachter*: "The Wehrmacht is what it has always been – pure inner-disciplined power – because of its leadership. It serves this state

Greyhounds of the Baltic Sea: A German speedboat.

Visiting the fleet in Kiel, 1934.

Wehrmacht Day in Nuremberg, 1935: motorized heavy artillery.

Hitler has given us tanks again.

Hitler inspects the first U-boats, August, 1935 in Kiel.

Hitler visiting the battleship "Schleswig-Holstein" in Hamburg harbor.

and affirms it with deepest conviction. It stands by the leadership that restored its distinguished right – not only as a weapon, but also as a champion of the unbounded trust of the people and of the state. Today, a sense of duty permeates the entire German nation. The power of the Wehrmacht flows from a strong belief in Germany and emblem of Germany's rebirth proudly on its helmet and uniform. The Wehrmacht stands with discipline and trust behind the leader of the state, the Führer of the Reich, Adolf Hitler, who came from our ranks and will always be one of us."

This is the real secret of the bond between the new army and the Führer. It is the same secret that

"Aviso Grille", a new ship in the navy that the Führer uses to visit the fleet.

Germany's right to life. Today's soldier is actively involved in the political life of this nation. Once again, the German people consider military service honorable. In Germany's period of darkness, the Wehrmacht passed the difficult test of discipline, sometimes under atrocious difficulties. Adolf Hitler took the fighting community in the trenches of the world war and made it the basis for a new national community. This became the foundation of a great tradition and the Wehrmacht, as heir of the old army, embraced it. The Wehrmacht is closely aligned with the nation and wears the unites the Führer and the worker, the Führer and the farmer, the Führer and the political fighters. All can say with conviction: He is one of us. The Führer comes from the farmer, he was a worker like millions and millions of his national comrades. He lay as a simple soldier in the trenches of a four-year battle for the homeland as did millions and millions of Germans. He was a soldier; a brave soldier who risked his life as a beacon in hellish crossfire. Today, when the old soldiers from the World War sit with the Führer, they reminisce about when they put their lives on the line for the Vaterland, an experience that holds them all together as comrades. They all know that when they swear allegiance to their comrade from the Great War they are honoring the legacy of all those who have fallen. It is this that makes the Wehrmacht a National Socialist organization from the inside: the Führer is their leader. He will always be a soldier ready to risk his own life in the face of the enemy. And as such, he has the right to lead others. He knows the needs and concerns of soldiers. He knows what soldiers want and what must be held back from them. This knowledge does not come from reports or stories, but from his own vast experience. It is clear that nothing makes the Wehrmacht more proud than to be bonded with this man today. When the troops parade before him, the eyes of the soldiers sparkle, they step more crisply, they tense every muscle. The leadership knows too that they have only Hitler to thank for the very existence of the Wehrmacht. It was Hitler's tough and exhausting political work that made it possible to re-establish German military might and to re-establish the traditional right of free German men to serve in the armed forces.

The Führer always impresses upon the young soldiers that this honor of serving the nation carries with it immense responsibility. He emphasizes his support of the Wehrmacht. He emphasizes to each soldier that without the sacrifices of the entire nation he would not be able to execute this honor and duty. After the glorious military parade at the 1935 party assembly in Nuremberg, the Führer said these eloquent words to his soldiers, "If you must make a personal sacrifice of obedience and duty, of subordination, hardship, stamina and performance, do not forget, my soldiers, that the entire German nation is also making a great sacrifice. We make this sacrifice with the conviction that we do not need war to get paid back. You truly need not glorify the German army; already glorious, you need only to protect it. Germany has not lost its military honor, particularly not in the last war. Take care that the nation can put its trust once again in the army because you wear the helmet of the army's most glorious times. Then the German nation will love you. The people will believe in their army and joyfully and happily sacrifice for it. The people will know that these sacrifices enable the army to protect the nation's peace and that the education of the German nation will be secure. This is the nation's plea, its hopes, and this is what the nation demands of you. And I know you will respond to this demand, these hopes, and this plea because you are new soldiers of the new German Reich."

The Führer and Wehrmacht, the Wehrmacht and the nation are one, as nation and Führer are one, united not only by an oath and a promise, but also by the common striving and common will for a free and strongly united National Socialist Reich.

The Führer visits Norwegian fjords on board a navy ship.

National Socialist Assembly: The nation's youngest drummers.

The Führer and German Youth
by Baldur von Schirach

Our young people honor the Führer in all parts of the Reich. Today the enthusiastic and enraptured youth who serve him and cheer him on is part of the very concept of Adolf Hitler. We take this for granted. Wherever the Führer is, children are too, proclaiming their loyalty to him. It doesn't matter if he is out driving on one of his trips past an unbroken honor guard comprised of these young people, or if they surround him like a wall with their parades and rallies at large, festive political events. That which is commonplace for us Germans never ceases to amaze foreigners. The mysterious connection between our nation's Führer and this young generation is an unaccountable phenomenon which foreigners call "The German Wonder." And indeed, what better way to describe the total unification of every class, trade, and religious denomination, in addition to all generations of our people. To us as Germans, it is also a wonder that the Führer could manage to get people of all ages to commit themselves to a common ideal, each in his or her own way, each trying to follow with his or her particular, individual strength.

The young and the youngest, with their passion and capacity for excitement, have always been the symbol of impetuous German youth; the elderly and the eldest are distinguished in years by their quiet clarity, constancy, and mature strength. Adolf Hitler raised an entire nation to serve this ideal. A ten-year old finds just as strong an awareness in shouldering his work and heralding his will decade after the Great War. It is pointless to ask who is to blame. Let me just say that the youth of those days is most definitely not to be solely blamed for the lack of respect and discipline. There were no role models for young people anywhere among the older generation. Because of

Reciting her poem. The Führer on one of his election campaign tours, 1932.

as a thirty-year-old or forty-year old. Yes, it is these very youth who feel particularly tied to the Führer because, with the unmistakable certainty of their instinct, they feel that the Führer has dedicated his thoughts and his concern to them all. They know that he serves the future that they themselves personify.

Particularly in the recent past Germany suffered terribly because of the conflicts between the younger and older generations. This conflict was especially tangible in every family during the

their personalities and actions, the so-called statesmen of the time were not able to evoke enthusiasm. They were either rejected or despised; so it was that inappropriate and false role-models such as film and sports stars remained. Is it the fault then of our young people that they were not able to fulfill the expectations of their elders?

Doesn't every educator know that more than anything young people must have heroic role models to demonstrate the proper way for a nation to develop? Men who served heroically in the World War could have been sustained by the youth. Instead the press and even influential men in the government ridiculed and insulted them. Unpunished, they were allowed to publicly deride the heroic ideal as stupid. In these circumstances, the war are still alive in our memories. These trials demonstrated to us with shocking clarity how trapped German youth can be when there is no leadership.

From the very first day, Adolf Hitler, through his works, tried to lead our youth back to itself. We

Again and again the Führer is seen surrounded by children. Right, Baldur von Schirach.

it is perfectly understandable that our youth lost all necessary standards and acceptable behavior. Because our young people observed so many people of the older generation behaving improperly, they held all of them in contempt. Cowardice was praised, and our youth believed everyone was a coward. The younger generation lost all sense of justice and injustice, boundaries and laws: the great court cases dealing with sexual issues brought against youth of that time as well as all the other juvenile crime during the years following can credit the success of this attempt, which not even the most optimistic ever expected, exclusively to Hitler's inexhaustible will power and persistence. The casual observer of the National Socialist movement's years of struggle overlooks all too easily the detailed work necessary to the movement that went along with the great slogans and slaughter. And the Führer was not simply handed the National Socialist Youth Movement as some believe. Nor did it emerge solely from newspaper appeals and speeches.

Young Germany greets the Führer in the election campaign.

Here, as in all areas of the movement, the Führer wrestled continuously year in and year out with draft laws until he was ready to announce the fundamental theorems with which his youth leaders would have to operate. A new chapter in the rearing of mankind began when Adolf Hitler coined the phrase, "Youth must lead youth." Only a genius could simultaneously close the door to the past and open the door to the future with one phrase. With this motto for education, Adolf Hitler won over the hearts of his nation's youth to his flag. It doesn't matter that hardly anyone understood the Führer's motto at first. Indeed, the fact that people ridiculed and disparaged it as simply another programmatic statement of the Führer is unimportant too – as is the fact that this law dictated the development of the Youth Movement and that this movement only included a few thousand members. Only one thing is all-important and significant: Adolf Hitler, empathic and in tune with the spirit of youth, set up and proclaimed a thesis that no other statesman or educator had been able to bring about. We felt even then that the largest youth movement in the world would grow from this tiny community.

With the exception of Adolf Hitler, all statesmen past and present have regarded leadership of the youth as the general responsibility of their own

Children's hands.

generation. They have seen youth exclusively from the point of view of the older generation. For them it was a given (about which they never gave a second thought) that the older generation was to take responsibility and leadership of the youth into its own hands.

This is the model that large state youth organizations in other lands follow. In contrast to all these earlier educational methods, Adolf Hitler has taken full responsibility for the outcome of his method. It was he who claimed responsibility as the educational authority. The fact that the German youth does not betray the Führer's trust can be linked to the stirring testimony of youth's inner value. Instead of betraying trust, the youth endeavors to justify as honor and duty, despite error and turmoil, this trust that they continue to feel. And so it is that they respect the Führer's mandates and painstakingly march forward, step by step, developing into a mighty organization – the envy of the world. And all of this without being compelled by a law, or a decree, but rather solely by the inner power of an influential idea. Envision what it means that, even before he came to power through the National Socialists, the Führer knew that the great majority of German youth was behind him. The Reich's Youth Day took place in Potsdam three months before the Führer was elected Chancellor, and it is still the largest

Hitler Youth as guests in Obersalzberg.

Munich, November 9, 1935. Before a festive reception into the party in front of the Braunes Haus.

youth march the world has ever seen. The Communist and Social-Democrat youth organizations were overpowered before January 30, 1933 – not by brutal violence, but rather because the National Socialists won the souls of its members through their ideas.

This greatly differentiates the Hitler Youth from the youth organizations of other countries: the Hitler Youth have not been allotted their responsibilities after the fact, but fought in the battle for power, sacrificed in this battle, and placed themselves in the spring of 1936 as volunteer followers whereby ten- and fourteen-year-old youngsters comprised well over 90% of all these youth.

National Socialist Assembly on the Strength of the Party, 1934. At the stadium with young people.

To this day, Adolf Hitler closely follows the work of his youth movement in all its facets. Year after year he receives in the chancellery the male and female winners of the Reich Vocational Competition in order to personally congratulate them. He inspects the miniature youth hostels the youngsters have built and looks at the plans they show him. He draws on his vast building experience to help them in word and deed. He often initiates contact by inviting a group of young people or a group handicrafts, hand-drawn postcards, needlework, and travel books. All of this expresses more eloquently than words how the thoughts of the younger generation encompass this man who gave them a sense of purpose and duty.

How often I have observed how the Führer tarried in front of these small and humble gifts rather than pausing at the costly and spectacular. These youngsters' birthday gifts seem to give him the most joy. They are, in truth and reality, made from

from the BDM over whom he met while traveling in Berchtesgaden or Berlin. He surprises them by serving coffee and cake while listening to them sing or tell of their travels. Perhaps the strongest expression of the unconditional relationship between the Führer and his youth is on his birthday. The long tables in the chancellery are covered with thousands of small gifts presented by boys and girls of the Reich with great care and the hope that their gifts will bring their Führer joy: the most precious material: from the love of the children that, as no one before him, Adolf Hitler feels so deeply.

The Hitler Youth carries the name of the Führer as part of its name. This bond between our nation's youth and the leader of our Reich symbolizes the deep inner bond between Adolf Hitler and the youngest of our nation. Today, once again, each girl and boy, as individuals and as a unit, is dedicated to one ideal and has a role model to whom

National Socialist Assembly, 1935, the Führer and our youth.

he or she is devoted and strives to follow. The German people can look to their future and see tranquillity. The fallacies of the past have been conquered. The time of generational problems is past. Although once youth groups of various political parties were wont to stand against each other in political controversy, today all stand as one front. Whereas, in the past, the poor and the rich were seen in a dismal clash of class, the present sees a faithful alliance of young people whose social awareness is stronger than any selfish desire. Herein is revealed the Führer's great educational power. What a short time ago appeared impossible and even a utopian claim is now a convincing reality. It is true that our young people have had to make sacrifices to bring about this reality. Some youth groups of the past in a sincere effort to achieve a greater goal have had to sacrifice in order to bring about a greater alliance of youth. The Hitler Youth, too, has had to lay some of its comrades in the bier in order to attain this inner oneness and unity. But without this unity, no community on earth can exist. The young people who died believing in the Führer and his forthcoming Reich, and the millions of young people still living are bound together in this same belief. They all feel that they carry the duty the Führer has placed upon them. They are one with him in serving the greatness of the Reich. Adolf Hitler's work is immortal because every German youngster stands ready to joyfully, dutifully, and loyally serve this cause his whole life long and to pass this on to those who come after him. This is how they will greet the next millennium.

After getting the Führer's autograph, she is lucky enough to be photographed with him, too.

The heroes of the movement, who were killed on the 9th of November 1923, were interred in the two Temples of Honor on Königsplatz in Munich on November 9, 1935.

The Führer and the National Socialist Movement
by Philipp Bouhler

When an anonymous soldier of the World War, who was temporarily blinded by mustard gas on November 8, 1918, decided, under the shattering impression of the miserable revolt in the stock market, to become a politician in order to intervene in the destiny of his nation, blinded to reason and humiliated, no one could have known that fourteen years later this same man would head the whole German nation as Führer and Reich's Chancellor. Only Adolf Hitler himself knew his own path, with the infallible belief that a genius has in his own power. But he also knew that even in chaotic postwar Germany, the political leadership would never go to a man who had neither reputation nor fame, title nor money. He could bring only his knowledge, his personality, and his belief in himself. He knew that the road to power in the state, which alone offered the possibility of changing Germany's hopeless situation, could only be taken by storm at the head of a movement, imbued with a triumphant idea and fanaticism, the nucleus of which in turn would have to be anchored by a strict organization.

Where would Friedrich the Great have been without the army he inherited from his father? It was this army that brought him his victories. Adolf Hitler, too, created an instrument that would be the very foundation of his politics. He created the NSDAP.

From very modest beginnings, he created this organization organically, an organization based on the idea of a Führer as absolute leader and a following of volunteers. This idea broke with all parliamentary traditions. Instead of the empty democratic principle of the equality of all men and majority rule, it gave absolute power and unlimited authority to the leadership. While German regional parliaments were bargaining for the personal advantages of separate cliques and exhausting themselves with fruitless votes regarding the vital problems of the German nation; while under the very eyes of the government, foreign elements were denigrating Germany's honor and reputation and spending the last monetary reserves of the German nation; and while the state stood by helpless and passive as the German fatherland stumbled ever more hopelessly into the abyss of political and economic slavery, Adolf Hitler was forging the instrument that would free Germany from within as well as from without.

For fourteen years, he steered his party around the obstacles. He worked tirelessly and doggedly to overcome danger. And finally, despite many setbacks, they began to celebrate success after success. Not because justice was on their side; justice can be perverted. Not because a devoted and fanatic following, trusting blindly, was fighting for the final victory; even the greatest sacrifices of property and blood can be for naught. Not because the opponents, driven by blind hatred and the will to destroy, made unimaginable mistakes. The movement was victorious because Adolf Hitler stood at its head, because he is the movement, because he personifies the idea of National Socialism.

Today Germany is free. The Germany of ignominy and shame, made a laughingstock in the eyes of the world by Jews and deserters, is gone. The years of slavery, inner strife, persecution, and oppression of the German in his own land, and the all-pervasive corruption in public life have vanished like a nightmare. The dream of centuries has become reality. A united German Reich has risen. Class hatred and snobbery have disappeared. There are no longer any political parties in Germany. United like brothers in striving to reach one single goal, the German tribes obey but one command.

All this is the work of Adolf Hitler. And if he had achieved no more than this – to reestablish Germany's ability to defend itself, this German nation that for one and a half decades had lain shattered and defenseless, at the mercy of its enemies – this alone would have been enough immortalize his name by carving it into the Parthenon [sic] of history.

A monument of honor in memory of those who fell at the Feldherrnhalle in Munich on the 9th of November 1923.

Think about it: the courage and trust, the infinite willingness to sacrifice, the devotion that thrived in the small group of faithful throughout all the long years of struggle, the group that grew and grew until it became a people's movement and finally an army of millions in the brown uniform of cherished most, say; "I am proud of this sacrifice?" Think about it. How was it possible to mold a single strong movement out of the jumble of parties and groups representing so many different interests, across differences in rank and class, across all religious denominations and opinions about how

National Socialist Assembly, 1934. Consecrating the flags.

honor. Think about it. Why did thousands happily and blindly obey his every signal for ten or more years, why did they put their professions and families last, why did they suffer mockery and scorn, why did they take insults, why did they donate their last, hard-earned penny without a word of complaint and without asking for thanks? Why did tens of thousands fall beneath the blows of their bestial enemies, and why did hundreds go to their death with a last "Heil Hitler" on their pale lips? Why did mothers, who had lost all they had and to structure the state. There is always but one answer: because Adolf Hitler was the leader of this movement. Brilliant organizer, fascinating speaker, and master of propaganda, dismissed by many an arrogant intellectual as a "political drummer," but who in reality was a born statesman, a daredevil with a burning heart who looked danger in the eye and faced it head on, a cool strategist who knew to wait until the hour had come. The leader who saw through the ruses of his opponents and took action against the wolves in sheep's clothing and

Re-creation of the historical march on the 9th of November 1934.

The first of the old comrades on the 9th of November 1935 in front of the Braunes Haus in Munich.

the sheep in wolves' clothing. The generous and kind man who is fond of everyone, who understands everyone and was always prepared to help when he could. He gave the movement its fundamental Weltanschauung, the quintessence of his political and philosophical knowledge, born in the hard years of his youth, years of learning and suffering, and purified and hardened in the heavy fire of the World War. He was and is the dynamic power that feeds the movement and drives it forward.

Rudolf Hess, when he opened the 1933 National Socialist Assembly victory party in Nuremberg, aptly and movingly described the unique bond that the movement shares with its Führer when he said, "My Führer! As leader of the party, you guaranteed our victory. When others stumbled, you remained upright. When others advised compromise, you remained unshakable. When others lost courage, you radiated new courage. When others left us, you took up the flag with more determination than before."

Adolf Hitler never thinks of himself. Determined to give his all, he marched away from the Bürgerbräukeller at the head of the procession that broke down in a hail of bullets next to the Feldherrnhalle. On that ill-fated morning in Wiessee, accompanied by just a few faithful companions, he arrested the traitors with his own hands. These are just two stories of many to exemplify the entire history of the party. A history that is one great example of the Führer's infinite devotion to his work and the unprecedented personal effort he gives it.

For him, there was no rest, no holiday. A fourteen- or sixteen-hour workday was not unusual for him.

National Socialist Assembly, 1934.

For nights on end he dictated, wrote proclamations, or designed flyers and posters. Then he would be off again by car, train, or airplane. His success as an orator is unparalleled as far as one can judge. He has held as many as four huge rallies in four different cities in a single day. There is no village, no town in which he does not recall menacing crowds of misguided Germans, distraught to the point of madness, following his car with dull murmuring, wild shouts, or even throwing stones, crowded masses showing him their love and devotion with roaring cries of "Heil Hitler" and a shower of flowers, overcrowded village taverns with several hundred people, or city assembly halls filled to bursting and with tens of thousands frenetically applauding his words, blond children lifted to his car by trusting mothers, or the modest light at an airfield shining like a guiding star after a frightening flight in the fog.

And once the decision had been made, when the election campaign was over, the Führer sat through the entire night with his faithful entourage next to the loudspeaker waiting for the results. Breathlessly, hearts beating faster, they listened to the reports. They took notes and made calculations, estimated results, and when the numbers surpassed even their most daring expectations, their jubilation knew no bounds.

There were also days with failures; there were setbacks. But the Führer never lost heart. Never did he allow his courage to fail. Even after unprecedented successes, his watchword was, "The struggle continues immediately!" especially if his projected goal had not yet been reached. After the November election in 1932, when compared to the previous election there was a drop in votes for the National Socialists, Adolf Hitler threw himself immediately and with determination – and it was long after midnight – into preparation for the next battle. He thought of ways to greatly increase the already vigorous propaganda activity in order to do better the next time around.

1935 National Socialist Assembly; with the workers on Zeppelinwiese.

On the 9th of November 1934 in front of Feldherrnhalle. The Führer with his deputy, Rudolph Hess, and the old comrades.

Sometimes Adolf Hitler's physical and emotional vigor seemed to go beyond what was humanly possible. Once he had just arrived at his hotel in Bayreuth in the early morning hours after a tiring night drive from Berchtesgaden when he received a telephone message about the mutiny crisis of SA-Führer Stennes in Berlin. The situation had already reached dangerous proportions. There was no stopping him. He got back in the car immediately and raced to Berlin. He held meetings and negotiated until evening and gave speeches to the SA-men on their premises. He returned to Munich that same

The fifteenth anniversary of the oldest town group of NSDAP in Rosenheim, 1925.

night, straight-away to the Braunes Haus from where the rebellion was finally quashed. For hours he dictated extemporaneously, his words immediately transcribed by typists: a special newspaper edition, appeals, flyers, meetings late into the night.

And again an attempt to split the movement failed.

This is Adolf Hitler.

Tireless work for the good of the movement, and constant worry about the fate of the movement have been Adolf Hitler's constant companions throughout the long years of struggle. This work, the continuous struggle, deprivation and sacrifice, and agonizing concern, has elevated him to colossal greatness as he now stands before Germany and the world.

Those who have seen the Führer in times of extreme difficulties, when the movement was at grave risk, know that this man is at his best when the moment demands lightning-fast action. They know too that there is no protective shelter for this man. At the moment of danger he will always be at the in the center of action leading his followers as he has in the past and as he will in the future.

Those who have seen the Führer during times like this also know that this man, whose eyes sparkle with unbounded kindness, becomes hard and relentless when his work is disrupted, when his movement is endangered.

No one is more generous than Adolf Hitler. He who has reestablished the right of German individualism does not want lackeys. He wants upright men around him, independent thinkers who act responsibly at their own discretion. He can accept frankness, and he has the superior insight to allow himself to be convinced by cogent logic. Because he has no use for bootlickers, but wants to promote independent thinking, he gives his collaborators the greatest possible freedom to act independently. He is a stranger to petty limitations or restrictions on the work of others. He sets up a basic course of action and points the direction, but he allows each individual the greatest possible leeway. He measures people by character and achievements, not by details of how and why and when, and not based on formulaic rubbish which he dislikes intensely. So he is always ready to forgive mistakes. He turns a blind eye when someone has erred or used poor judgment. With great patience and forbearance, he overlooks personal flaws and inadequacies knowing they are part of human nature.

But woe is him who tries to shake the foundations of the movement! Woe is him who dares to sin

An old soldier: The Führer congratulates General Litzmann (now deceased) on his birthday.

against the spirit of the movement or to destroy the nature of the organization! Woe is him who has sworn loyalty to the Führer and to the movement and who breaches it. Disloyalty will not be pardoned. No one is spared. In this case rank and name make no difference. In this case merit, no matter how great, does not weigh enough; the scales tip and the offender falls back into the void from whence he came.

As a mountaineer who has arduously reached the steep summit of a mountain looks down at the winding, stony path, through hills and valleys, today Adolf Hitler, Germany's Führer, can look back upon the path, fourteen years of struggle for an unprecedented rise to the position of leader of a nation, fourteen years replete with danger, sacrifice, and tribulation, but also with trust, happiness, and proud satisfaction.

National Socialist Freedom Assembly. The Führer awaits the brown columns.

And Adolf Hitler looks back often. He is richly blessed with a trait common in all truly great men: gratitude. Gratitude for providence which time and time again has seemed to work in mysterious, incomprehensible ways, providence which fortunately pointed to the one right path; gratitude to his movement and to his fellow fighters who were true to him through thick and thin. He knows all these men personally, he is sincerely pleased for the opportunity to shake hands with these men when he runs into them unexpectedly out in the country. And they can always count on him to listen to what they have to say. There is a particularly warm comradeship between him and his old SA- and SS-men. The soldier in Hitler has always found the right words for fighting party troops trained in the spirit of true soldiers. Since the National Socialist Party was a movement of soldiers from the very beginning, it drew fighting men to it like a magnet. In the early days of the movement, when the SA was slowly emerging from the troopers of the party, which consisted of only a handful of the Führer's war comrades, Adolf Hitler spent a great deal of time in their midst. He demonstrated with them in the streets; he went with them to their opponents' rallies where his heckling always hit the target. When they marched outside cities, he shared with them the straw pallets of their quarters; when the Red mob in Coburg crowded howling around the SA, he stood in the midst of the thickest throng and delivered many a powerful blow himself.

It is no wonder that even today, as Reich's Chancellor, he feels comfortable among his old comrades. How often has he been best man at their weddings, how often has he thrilled fellow party members by agreeing to be their sons' godfather. How often has he hospitably entertained SA-comrades in his house or received them in the chancellery. And how often has he even gone to them when they have met for the traditional, simple commemoration celebrations in restaurants or in the mess hall of the Braunes Haus. Whenever the old and young, all in their brown shirts and ever radiant in his presence, sat around him, Adolf Hitler was as ever one of their own, a comrade among comrades.

More than anything else, it is this human side that has etched a picture of the Führer upon millions of hearts. People can always be forced to obey. But because of this man's extraordinary achievements, our nation voluntarily and gladly shows its respect to the man leading it. No power on earth could force the people to support the Führer with this

The 1923 'Bloody Flag' at the National Socialist Assembly in Nuremberg.

The 9th of November 1935 in Munich. The Führer speaks with a party member, the widow of a man who fell on the 9th of November 1923. Braunes Haus in the background.

love and devotion, nor is it a product of pure chance. And it is rooted in the personality of Adolf Hitler. His personality pulls the people powerfully under his spell, and once they have sensed even a hint of his spirit it never lets them go. His personality is a source of courage for the timid, strength for the weak, and fresh hope for those who are desperate.

But just as Adolf Hitler continues to pump impetus and strength to the movement, just as his spirit and blood flow and pulse through this huge body of the party, the movement in turn continues to be a source strength for him.

The movement is his homeland. It is the soil in which his whole being is rooted. Just as it is impossible to imagine the National Socialist Movement without Adolf Hitler, so it is impossible to imagine the Führer without the movement. It is with this movement that he first developed the fundamental principles which made it possible for him to take the rudder of German destiny and put his ideas and plans into action one after another. In addition, the movement and his preoccupation with it have filled his life to such an extent that he would not be able to live without it. Even though the time-consuming but fulfilling business of Adolf Hitler the statesman leaves him little time to deal with matters of the party, he takes as much interest as he always has in everything that goes on within the whole organization. He remains in constant contact with the men who are in leadership positions within the party. When visiting ministers of the Reich or a Gau, or top leaders in the SA or the SS, or when youth organizations come to Berlin, the Führer invites them to be his guests in the chancellery.

When he is tired and weary, contact with the movement revitalizes him. When he steps up to the podium at National Socialist rallies and begins to speak, when he sees thousands of trusting eyes trained expectantly on him, then the spark that leapt from him to the masses leaps back to him, renewing his vigor and filling him with an increased desire for action. This constant current running back and forth between Führer and followers, this effect on others that reflects back to him, is perhaps the final mystery of Adolf Hitler's success and of the success of the National Socialist Movement.

This bond of destiny for better or for worse between Führer and movement explains why Adolf Hitler is drawn as if by magic to the historical sites of the movement, to those well-known places which for him are linked for all time to indelible memories. And sometimes perhaps he feels slightly melancholy as he thinks about the past, of a time

A historical sight. The Führer and Dr. Goebbels visit the room in the Sterneckerbäu that served as the first office of the party in 1920.

when it was still difficult to be a National Socialist! In an unprepossessing corner of the street, Sterneckergäßchen, in Munich there is an old house with the little dark room that had served as the party office in the early days of the movement. After seizing power, the Führer requested that it be returned to its old condition and preserved for posterity. Some time later when Chancellor Adolf Hitler entered this broom closet of a room in the Sterneckerbräus after a get-together in the adjacent Leiber Room with his old guard, he found on the walls the very same red posters he had used to appeal to the people of Munich to come to the NSDAP rallies.

Those large, red posters contained nothing but text, rousing manifestos designed to clear the way for the opinion of the people previously poisoned by Marxism. Those posters drew increasing crowds of people around Munich's kiosks, until the police finally banned them, ostensibly for "logistical reasons." In this room Hitler found the first flyers he had written and used relentlessly to get even with all the enemies of the German nation. He picked up the cigar box that had substituted for a safe in those times when everything was so scarce, and old images came alive and drifted through his mind. In this room, where there is practically no daylight, he had sat while doggedly fighting to get his way within the committee of the new party. All of them meant well, but it was very difficult to convince them that if the movement were going to cross swords with Marxism, it needed the ear of the public, more precisely the ear of the workers, the "proletariat." And to be successful they would have to use propaganda.

Preparing for the National Socialist Party Assembly in 1935. The Führer discussing the order of the procession.

And in the end reason won. Adolf Hitler's popularity constantly increased and there was no arguing that his strategies had been successful. And so the young party was not forgotten, it did not slowly die like a meaningless club. It became a movement, filling more and more people with its concepts until by and by Germany had a new face- because now it had a Führer.

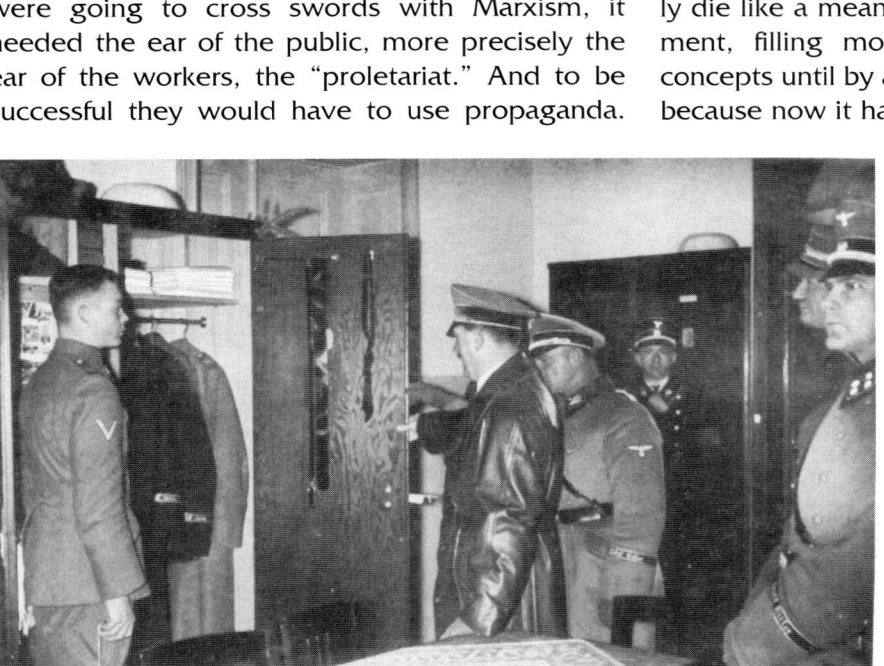

November 9, 1933 was the tenth anniversary of the day on which Adolf Hitler had made a desperate attempt to change Germany's destiny. Dejected and defenseless the fatherland faced a world of enemies. Torn apart from within, powerless and without a common goal, Germany was at the mercy of rebels greedy for booty. There was a kind of method to the madness of inflation that was driving the country inexorably toward catastrophe. Like hyenas, although disguised as the bourgeois, separatists sneaked throughout the country and waited for the right moment to realize their dark goals and

Adolf Hitler visiting his personal guard. SS General Josef Dietich stands next to Hitler.

Visit to Landsberg Prison, 1934.

Consecration of the flags and honoring the dead, 1935.

destroy the German Reich for good. If action were not taken now, it would be forever too late. And Adolf Hitler acted. The attempt failed, the uprising fell apart – not only because of the shameful traitors, disgraced forever. Now, ten years later, the Führer realizes that this failure was actually a stroke of luck. If the coup had been successful, would the movement, which had no resources at the time, have been able to fulfill its task? The concept of National Socialism had not yet permeated the German nation. The people had not yet grasped its meaning. It would not have been possible yet for a spiritual revolution to penetrate everything. A new Weltanschauung to completely replace the old system could not have followed radical political change. It takes more than idealism to build a state.

The time was not yet right. The movement did not yet have the necessary prerequisites to take over a state. And yet it was necessary to march in Munich on the ninth of November. It was necessary that the first victims of the movement lose their lives at the Feldherrnhalle. And the seed that was planted by the blood of the fallen grew and bore fruit in all of Germany.

The inspiring celebration on this important day in the history of the movement and for the whole German nation put all of Munich under a spell. The old comrades-in-arms spent the night before in the historical hall in the Bürgerbräukeller where the uprising had begun. It was here that the Führer with his storm troopers had forced his way into a patriotic demonstration during Bavarian Commissar von Kahr's speech. It was here that Hitler had proclaimed the revolution. The bullet hole of the shot he had fired at the ceiling with his handgun as a signal was still visible. It was here that Kahr, Lossow and Seisser had given their word to take part in the new national government, only to despicably go back on their word just a few hours later. The Führer commemorated that great moment and then gave a retrospective of the years that followed, the years of struggle, struggle, and more struggle that had finally led to victory. For a long time afterward Adolf Hitler sat with his men exchanging words, greetings, and glances.

The next morning he gathered his comrades-in-arms around him again. They lined up just as they had ten years before. Everyone wore a simple brown shirt. Just like that day, the historical procession came together at the Ludwigsbrücke and marched through the decorated streets of the city to the Feldherrnhalle. On the Odeonsplatz stood, surrounded by a closely packed crowd of people, interminable rows of brown and black columns of

The 9th of November, 1935 at the Königsplatz in Munich. The Führer's personal guard.

SA and SS. Standard bearers stood in front. It was an unforgettable scene as the procession came closer. The Führer, himself deeply moved, spoke emotionally in memory of the first victims of the German revolution. Then he walked with measured steps down the stairs of the Feldherrnhalle and stepped up to the newly built monument of honor about to be unveiled. It was breathtaking as he let the large wreath slide down the marble plaque. The touching greeting on the wreath to those who had fallen said: "And still you were victorious!" Ever since this solemn hour, two steel-helmeted SS honor guards stand day and night on either side of the monument. Everyone passing by reverently raises an arm in German greeting. In ensuing years as well, this day has been celebrated ceremoniously, and it is the will of the Führer that this will be so forevermore.

SS Generalmajor Julius Schaub, one of the Führer's oldest comrades-in-arms and a constant companion, tells the following story about a visit to Landsberg Prison ten years after the Führer and his faithful men had been held there for over a year: "After a truly heroic struggle leading to the national revolution breakthrough, the Führer wanted to visit Landsberg Prison on the Lech River where he had spent over a year and where he wrote most of his book "Mein Kampf."

On the afternoon of October 7, 1934, one of those clear, sunny days that only comes in the fall, we drove to Landsberg by car. The Führer, the present Municipal Administrator of Munich and SS-Officer Maurice, and I all sat in the car. All three of us had been imprisoned at Landsberg together.

The autumn wind tossed the leaves as we drove through Pasing, past the Ammersee, and further into Bavarian Swabia. Shortly before we reached Landsberg, we stopped briefly at a firebreak in the woods. The car accompanying ours was sent ahead to announce the unexpected visit of the Führer to the prison so that we could drive up to the prison without causing a stir.

As we drove, memories of those early days in Landsberg returned. And the closer we got to the town, the more vivid the images were as we recalled the experiences we had had as prisoners ten years before. Names such as Hess, Kriebel, Weber, Kallenbach, Fischer, and Frösch came to mind. We spoke of Mufti. This is what the prisoners in Landsberg called the prison warden who was the master of our fate in Landsberg. And as the gates and walls of the marvelous old town appeared in the distance, the Führer told us how he had been released in 1924 a few days before Christmas, how Adolf Müller had picked him up in an old Benz, and how his photograph had been taken next to the car in front of the gate.

We drove through the gate slowly into town, on a

The Führer at the National Socialist Freedom Assembly. Inspecting the honor company of his personal guard.

National Socialist formations on the 9th of November, 1935 on the almost completed Königsplatz.

SA motorcade escorting the Führer at the National Socialist Assembly, 1935.

Photograph taken while imprisoned at Landsberg Prison in 1924.   *The Führer returns ten years later. At the window of his former cell.*

At a conference during the days of struggle. The Führer takes a few notes while listening to a speaker.
From left to right in the front row: Hess, Rust, the Führer, Zörner, Kerrl. 2nd row: Schreck, sitting behind Hess.

The Führer surrounded by his closest colleagues the night of the Reichstag Election, March 29, 1936.

narrow, steep street down to the lovely market place. Our visit was so unexpected that very few people on the street recognized the Führer. We drove on through town and crossed the bridge over the Lech. Then on our right we could see the roofs of the prison complex sitting in the landscape there like a small fortress, built in the traditional shape of a star. A narrow road, past a development, leads to the prison entrance. As soon as they had heard about the Führer's arrival, the wives and children of the prison officials had alerted one another and came with bouquets of flowers they had hurriedly picked from their gardens.

Then the Führer got out and walked through the great portal which he had first entered on November 11, 1923.

The prison officials, some of whom had been here since that time, were obviously deeply moved by this reunion. Huge key rings clattered. It was the same melody we had heard in the tedious monotony of imprisonment as our days in the narrow cells slipped by and the "lights out" order was given. Doors closed and then the steps of the jailer could be heard moving ever further down the corridor.

Slowly the Führer, with Maurice and me at his side, strode down the path he had walked hundreds of times ten years before. Many ideas had come to him here, ideas which had in the meantime taken shape and become reality. We walked around the prison's church, past one of the prison wings, in those days filled with the men of Hitler's combat patrol because the prison had been so over occupied.

The main part of the prison is behind the wing connected to it by a low, two-story building. As we rounded the corner, the Führer instinctively stopped for a moment. One of the windows above belonged to cell number seven where he had lived for a year.

An official had preceded us, and he opened the narrow door leading into the corridor of the prison. There were flowers on the table and garlands wound around the doors. This wing of the prison is no longer used, but it remains as a historical monument, an outward sign that chains cannot kill the spirit. It is a reminder that, while they were in prison, the very men who were supposed to have been destroyed drew strength to begin the struggle anew and to fight to a victorious end. A narrow staircase leads up to the second floor where the Führer, Rudolf Hess, Lieutenant Colonel Kriebel and the leader of the Oberlandbund, Dr. Weber, had been housed.

The doors to the separate cells all open on a corridor. Above cell number seven is a plaque commemorating the Führer's imprisonment there. On the table is a visitors' book, where the Führer, ten years after he had left Landsberg, signed his name boldly. He spent a long time in his former cell. As he stood at the window through which he had so often looked over the walls into the Swabian countryside, Heinrich Hoffmann recorded this historical visit with a photograph. And he showed us a photograph that had been taken from the same spot ten years earlier.

The Führer now went out to the other part of the prison, to the visitors' room, where he had often been visited by his old comrades-in-arms, who were keeping the organization going on the outside and who had created a small but powerful Greater German troop which he would later depend on.

The sun was setting as the Führer strode out into the courtyard. Everything was as it had been. Out of reverence nothing had been changed. Along the wall is a narrow path that has been named

Adolf Hitler Path. While other prisoners had spent their time playing loud games, the Führer had walked up and down this path, deep in thought or engrossed in conversation with a comrade.

By the time we reached the gate, it was twilight. The old prison officials who still had not composed themselves and were speechless upon seeing that the man they had guarded so long ago stood before them now as the Führer of the Reich. The Führer said a warm good-bye to them.

In the meantime, in Landsberg the rumor had raced from person to person; the Führer is here. When we returned to town it was overflowing with people who wanted to take advantage of this opportunity to see the Führer. The car could make its way only very slowly through the cheering crowds. Closely packed, they crowded around filling the market place, and the narrow, steep street to the gate. What a reunion it was! Ten years before, the prisoners had secretly published a small, satirical newspaper titled "The Landberg Freeman." Now, ten years later, this title was reality: former prisoner Adolf Hitler had become the free man of the town of Landsberg and the whole population cheered him on!

The Führer with the Labor Corps at Zeppelinfeld in Nuremberg. National Socialist Assembly, 1935.

We stopped again on the hill in front of the gate where on a cold, gray winter's day a photograph had been taken of the Führer next to Adolf Müller's car to mark the beginning of a new phase in his life. And Heinrich Hoffmann recorded this moment with his camera too.

In the meantime, the twilight had darkened and we drove toward evening, back to Munich. We were silent in the car. Each one of us, filled with the great events of the last ten years, in the grip of the wonderful change that had taken place, pursued his own thoughts. Much that had been born in quiet loneliness was now reality. And over prison walls, the German people had received the most marvelous gift from the Führer: freedom.

The Führer has always shown a special interest in the NSDAP Assemblies. They have always been the a showplace for all to see the greatness and the unity of the movement. There is always a large military parade drawing together comrades in brown shirts from all over Germany. They were, and still are, the benchmarks of development and growth of the movement. The first National Socialist Assemblies in Munich in January 1923 were more or less local events. But the second, three and a half years later in Weimar, showed Germany and the world that the movement which had been declared dead was alive. And it was gathering strength to rise again. The fact that Adolf Hitler declared that Dürer's old historical city of Nuremberg would forever be the city of National Socialist Assemblies after the 1927 and 1929 congresses had been held there is characteristic of the Führer's desire, expressed over and over again, to give the movement a sense of tradition.

The Führer always felt an inner need to be involved in every preparatory detail for each National Socialist Assembly. In the days of the struggle he went deeply into debt to make it possible for as many SA-men as possible to participate. He himself always made decisions regarding the details of the programs. It was Hitler himself who provided the guidelines for various special conferences where presentations and specific discussions in areas such as youth concerns, women's concerns, students' concerns, and local politics were dealt with. He always personally supervised the extensive preparations necessary for transporting, housing, and feeding the masses. Organizing special trains, preparing mass quarters, distributing deliveries of food for the crowds, and later purchasing special field kitchens – these all became more and more important as the National Socialist Assemblies grew to be major productions. The Führer and his staff are often in Nuremberg to supervise preparation on the spot. And then the curtain rises and the powerful drama unfolds before the eyes of the enthusiastic crowd. The framework always remains the same, but each time it presents new impressions of incredible beauty and power. It has been a simple matter of honor that the Führer always make it possible for a number of the oldest party members and the survivors of fallen soldiers to be present with great numbers of other guests of honor at these celebrations.

Of course the Führer could not begin to restructure the National Socialist Assemblies completely in accordance with his wishes until after the revolution achieved victory. First the great square in Luitpoldhain was rearranged according to his requirements. The intention here was to make room for SA and SS formations and consecration of the flags. Soon afterward a huge grandstand overshadowed by a gigantic eagle was built on Zeppelinfeld where great processions of political leaders have taken place since 1933.

In the meantime this tremendous project for the future, initiated by the Führer, has begun, and it will be completed in eight years. This will be a cultural monument to the National Socialist movement. The impressive size of this project will show future generations the victorious, all-powerful concept embodied in these proud buildings.

A whole new city is being built on the National Socialist rally grounds southeast of Nuremberg. It will have its own water supply and electricity works, and its own sewage system making it completely independent of the city of Nuremberg. Tent cities will be built on the huge camping ground providing accommodations for up to 500,000 people. The Congress Hall, the cornerstone of which is just now being laid, will hold 65,000 people. A special field large enough for 400,000 spectators will be set aside for Wehrmacht's demonstrations. Wide roads leading to the area and a special railroad station will provide smooth transportation for the crowds of people. And finally an 80-90 meter-wide road running through Dutzendteich on a huge dam will be built for parades. A special association has been founded with representatives of the party, the state, the German Reich's railroad, and the city of Nuremberg to guarantee uniform completion of this tremendous task.

Once this work is complete, the Nationalist Socialist Assembly will concentrate on a complete display of the strength National Socialist Germany. It will truly become the Reichstag of the German nation. The Führer is following the progress of this momentous project with joyous pride and heartfelt interest.

Years ago the Führer said: "Soon I will have to go to Berlin, because Berlin is the center of political life. But the seat of the movement will always remain Munich." And he has kept his word about Munich. Braunes Haus has come to represent something special in the whole world and has become a symbol of National Socialism. Near the housing departments of the Reich's leadership two massive buildings are being built, the Führer

Building and the Administration Building, as a visible statement of the Führer's will. The Führer himself, who still keeps an apartment in Munich, returns as often as possible. It has become a second home for him and whenever possible he stays at Braunes Haus where he used to work. The leaders of the Reich meet here for conferences and important party discussions take place here too.

And finally, the Führer has officially dubbed Munich the "City of the Movement" as a way of immortalizing the bond between the party and this city. This gift is in gratitude to Munich for the early political successes there, for the sacrifices Munich made for the sake of the movement, and for the loyalty the city has shown him.

Munich is the birthplace of the movement.

It was here that the movement proved its right to exist.

It was here that the first demonstrations took place, beginning modestly and gradually growing into mass rallies on a grand scale.

It was in the meeting halls here that the first battles and the first violent clashes with the Marxists took place.

The ground in front of the Feldherrnhalle is sanctified by the blood of the first martyrs of the National Socialist concept.

It was here that the great trial took place bringing Adolf Hitler's name to the attention of the world for the first time.

It was here that the NSDAP was founded for the second time in a historical place.

It was from here that the NSDAP began its triumphal march through all of Germany.

Adolf Hitler has never been a party leader in the usual sense, just as the NSDAP has never been a party like other parties. It has always been only the organizational center of the great National Socialist Movement. It is the National Socialist Movement that is the sole representative of the political will of the German nation.

From the very beginning, the task of the NSDAP was to absorb the many other parties, to get rid of the diversity of parties in Germany, and to replace them with a single national community. Adolf Hitler never saw the NSDAP as an end in itself. He always saw it as nothing more than the active center of the German nation. Beyond the NSDAP is the higher goal of his yearning – the goal he has fought for and worked for and cared for:

"Germany, and Germany alone!"

The Führer consecrates flags at the National Socialist Assembly.